A WORLD MADE WHOLE

The Rediscovery of the Celtic Tradition

Esther de Waal

Fount

An Imprint of HarperCollins*Publishers*

First published in Great Britain in 1991 by Fount Paperbacks

Fount Paperbacks is an imprint of
HarperCollins Religious Division,
part of the HarperCollins Publishing Group
77–85 Fulham Palace Road, London W6 8JB

Printed and bound in Great Britain by HarperCollins Manufacturing, Glasgow

A catalogue record for this book is available from the British Library

Books by the same author

available as
Fount Paperbacks

SEEKING GOD

LIVING WITH CONTRADICTION

A World Made Whole

Esther de Waal read history at Cambridge and has since taught history at Cambridge and Nottingham Universities, for Lincoln Theological College and for the Canterbury School of Ministry, and has been a tutor with the Open University for over fifteen years. Under her maiden name, Esther Moir, she has written books and articles on history and architecture. In 1984, when living in Canterbury, she wrote *Seeking God, the Way of St Benedict* (Fount), which has been published in America and translated into French, Dutch, Italian and German. In 1985 she was given an honorary doctorate from St John's Collegeville, Minnesota, for her contribution to Benedictine studies and for her ecumenical work.

Her other interest is in Celtic spirituality, and her books on the subject include *God under my Roof: Celtic Songs and Blessings* (SLG Press, Fairacres, Oxford, 1984) and *The Celtic Vision, Selections from the Carmina Gadelica* (Darton, Longman & Todd, 1988). With A. M. Allchin she edited *Threshold of Light: Prayers and Praises from the Celtic Tradition* (Darton, Longman & Todd, 1986).

For HIROE
my grandson who belongs to two worlds

CONTENTS

Introductory Note

I have written this book with one purpose and one hope, and that is that it will encourage others to discover for themselves some of the riches that I have myself found in the Celtic tradition. It has not been easy to write, for much of the material was available only in scholarly editions or learned journals where the emphasis was antiquarian, linguistic or ethnographical, but showed little concern for how it might relate to Christian understanding or make a contribution to daily life. I have tried to avoid two extremes, on the one hand making it so academic that it appears remote and irrelevant, and on the other hand reading into it what we want to find. While I have tried to remain true to the original material I hope that I have managed to present it in a way that will enable the readers to encounter it, and engage with it for themselves, so that it becomes life-giving on their own Christian journey. That is the reason that I have given comparatively little historical background or context. The notes and references are included for those readers who want to pursue the subject further, but the book can just as well be read without them. My concern has rather been to present the subject in terms of a succession of themes with which readers can identify from their own experience. Here is the Celtic way of seeing the world. It cannot be understood only in cerebral terms; it speaks to the heart, it is closer to poetry, and, like poetry, it must remain ultimately elusive.

> You can come in
> You can come a long way . . .
> But you won't be inside.

These lines from R.S. Thomas, the contemporary Welsh poet, are a very salutary warning about believing that we can ever actually really know, understand, let alone possess another world. While we welcome the Celts as brothers and sisters we do them a disservice if we allow ourselves to forget that the saints and hermits, the ordinary men and women who figure in these pages are also strangers. We stand on the fringe of their world, grateful for what we can see, but we must never forget that it is ultimately mystery, to be handled with reverence.

Many places and many people have contributed to the making of this book. I owe much to conversations with the Rev. Canon A.M. Allchin, the Rev. and Mrs Saunders Davies, the Rev. James Coutts. Sr Barbara M.M.M. first took me to Monasterboice and other places in Ireland. I have corresponded with many people whose names I shall not attempt to enumerate. Christine Whitell of Marshall Pickering, who first suggested this book, has been a constant source of encouragement. But one person in particular has haunted me while I have been writing this book and that is Nora Chadwick. Many years ago, long before I was seriously interested in things Celtic, I lived in her house in Cambridge, and I have often thought of her since, with her books and her harps, and her quiet, profound, scholarly presence. Something that she wrote explaining her dedication to the subject has remained with me, and I make it my own apologia too. "Shall I confess the truth? I have chosen it because of its lasting beauty."

Cwm Cottage   8th July 1990
Rowlestone
Pontrilas
Herefordshire

Preface

My discovery of the Celtic really began with place. But there was in addition the accident of birth, for I come from a Scottish family of Moirs who can trace their ancestry back for centuries to the east coast of Scotland, though in childhood this meant little more than living under the eye of portraits of forebears of stern and forbidding appearance. My own upbringing was set in the gentle, rolling green Shropshire hills of the Welsh border country, somewhat apart therefore from the mainstream of English life. Borderlands are ambiguous places in which different cultures and traditions meet, frontiers from which the new can open up. Perhaps I took all this a little for granted and did not really think much about it at all. It was in fact one September evening, several years ago, when I was staying in Ireland and was taken to see the high crosses at Monasterboice, that I now look back to as the moment of true conversion.

Familiarity with the outline of the traditional Celtic cross, a circle imposed on the cross, which I had seen illustrated time and again, had not prepared me for the actual experience of finding myself standing in front of a high cross twelve or fourteen feet tall. The image is a powerful one, the great O of creation, the circle of the world, and the cross of redemption brought together into one whole. I was being confronted here for the first time with a starkly dramatic statement of what I was to find time and again as I came to understand better the Celtic way of seeing the world: this ability to hold things together. Here the cross makes a simple statement about the interconnection of redemption and creation, that we cannot have the light without the dark, that the two are interdependent. And then, as I drew closer, I could see that on each side the crosses were covered with intricately carved panels which told of God at work in history: biblical scenes of the story of salvation, which converged on the two central representations of the judgement and the crucifixion. The suffering portrayed in the figure of the crucified Christ was quite extraordinary – but then sometimes (though not always) the image spoke further: this same crucified Christ was shown wearing a long tunic, so that he was simultaneously the dying Saviour and the risen Lord: Christ in death and in resurrection. Again I was finding this extraordinary gift of juxtaposing two things. And then as I raised my eyes to the top of the cross I found my curiosity further aroused. For the two figures in the dominant top panel were none other than St Antony of Egypt and St Paul of Thebes. Why, I asked myself, should the men who carved these crosses in the tenth century choose to give this place of honour to two hermit saints of the Egyptian desert?

I came a little nearer to an answer when sometime later I made a pilgrimage to Disserth, a tiny church beside a stream in a remote wooded valley in mid-Wales. This is one of the many spots that can still be found throughout Ireland and Wales, the Dysarts and Disserths, originally the isolated places in woods and valleys, on rocky cliffs and lonely islands, which were the homes of the early hermits. Here, though admittedly in a rather different landscape, the eremitical way of life of the Egyptian desert was lived out in a Celtic setting.

The following year on a visit to Iona I met Lord George MacLeod, the man who has dedicated himself to rebuilding St Columba's abbey and making it a place of pilgrimage known now throughout the world. As we walked together round the cloisters, he spoke of how urgent he felt it was that people should find again the living tradition of the Celtic world. "Everyone today keeps asking, 'What is the matter?' ", he said, "and the short answer is MATTER is the matter. It is our view of matter, the extent to which the Church has spiritualized the faith and set it apart from the material world, that has brought us where we are today." If only we were to stop and to take hold once again of the Celtic understanding of the world and creation, he added, we would find such an attitude challenged and corrected. The world is God's world and he is known in and through it. This is what Professor John Macquarrie would agree is most characteristic: "the profound sense of the immanence of God in the world . . . the sense of an all-pervading presence".[1] This is an approach to life in which God breaks in on the ordinary, daily, mundane, earthy. It is very much a down-to-earth spirituality. The sense of the presence of God informs daily life and transforms it, so that any moment, any object, any job of work, can become the time and the place for an encounter with God. It is ultimately a question of vision, of seeing. So the Celtic approach to God opens up a world in which nothing is too common to be exalted and nothing is so exalted that it cannot be made common. As an old woman in Kerry, in the southwest of Ireland, says, "Heaven lies a foot and a half above the height of a man." There is nothing here of that Puritan legacy which has hung so heavily over much British and American religion, which seems to insist on the superiority of the spiritual and says that all that has to do with the body must be trampled on and denied.

This sense of acclaiming God in and through the world of his creating, and in and through the material things of daily life, was brought home to me on another occasion which was to prove extremely significant. I had picked up a book on prayer by Etta Gullick, but I got no further than the early pages when I was arrested by a quotation that she used. It was a blessing of the fire by a Hebridean woman as she lifted the peats at the start of the day. The night before she would have banked down the fire, making the action a rhythmic one and using at the same time a threefold commendation to the Trinity to watch and to guard her household. Now at the start of a new day she brought that fire to life again, and as she did so said:

> I will kindle my fire this morning
> In the presence of the holy angels of heaven,

As the embers burst into flame she made that flame of fire symbolic of the flame of love which she would keep burning for herself, for her family, for her kin, for her enemies, for the whole world.

> God, kindle thou in my heart within
> A flame of love to my neighbour,
> To my foe, to my friend, to my kindred all.
> To the brave, to the knave, to the thrall . . .
> Without malice, without jealousy, without envy
> Without fear, without terror of anyone under the sun.

There was an immediacy and an earthiness here that greatly attracted me. It sent me off on a further trail in pursuit of Alexander Carmichael and of the six volumes of invocations, poems, prayers and blessings that he had collected in the Scottish Highlands and the Outer Hebrides at the end of the last century.[2] He was himself a quite extraordinary man, for throughout his life he worked in customs and excise in Edinburgh, but yet spent every possible spare moment travelling throughout Scotland to find and preserve for posterity this material, passed down by oral tradition from generation to generation. A considerable poet himself, he also made sensitive translations from the original Gaelic into English. Later on I found the almost parallel work of Douglas Hyde in Ireland, done not only about the same time but also curiously enough by another man in public life.[3] In some strange way I found this reassuring, for nobody could begin to see this as the work of escapist, romantic Celtic enthusiasts beguiled by some elusive "Celtic twilight".

Indeed the more deeply that I came to know this way of seeing the world the further I found any idea of "Celtic twilight" began to recede. The tendency in late nineteenth-century artistic and literary circles to portray a half-lit, strangely brooding, melancholy and romantic Celtic world, became increasingly unconvincing. The dangers of sentimentality can all too easily haunt any attempt to rediscover the Celtic past, and it is only too tempting to impose upon the past one's own preconceptions and expectations. To allow this world to reveal its secrets, to get to know and to understand its hidden treasures requires time, as Giraldus Cambrensis discovered as long ago as the twelfth century. It was in 1185 that this Welsh traveller and chronicler first saw the Book of Kells. Look superficially, he said, and you will miss it, it will elude you. Look more carefully and then you will penetrate to its heart. "You will make out intricacies, so delicate and so subtle, so exact and compact, so full of knots and links, with colours as fresh and vivid, that you might say all this was the work of an angel, not of a man . . . For my part, the oftener I see the book, and the more carefully I study it, the more I am lost in ever fresh amazement, and I see more and more wonders . . ." David Jones, the great Welsh poet and artist of our own day, used an apt phrase in speaking of the secrets of the Celtic world, "an elusive hardness", a phrase which seems to me to catch the sharpness and clarity that Giraldus Cambrensis had found. Illuminated manuscripts and artefacts were now adding to my understanding of the riches of the world that I was encountering. The book of Kells and the book of Durrow, the Armagh chalice and the Derrynaflan hoard, drew me not only by their extraordinary beauty and by the depths and the intricacy of their designs but also by the sense of harmony and integration which underlay the complexity of their intertwining spirals and whorls and scrolls. I was made aware yet again of how unique this was, unparalled by anything I had seen before.

Gradually the truth was dawning on me that I was being presented with a form of Christianity which was in many ways very different from that which I had hitherto known. Here was a Christianity which was not Mediterranean-based, but forged anew on the fringes of Europe by a people who knew nothing of Rome or of urban civilization. It came out of a rural people, a hierarchical, tribal-based society in which personal relationships were of paramount importance – not only relationships between people, but relationships with the wild creatures and with material things, and not least, between this world and the next. It came out of a people who were not afraid to carry over their earlier pagan, pre-Christian beliefs into Christianity and fuse the old with the new. It was deeply influenced by the east, drawing much into its monasticism from the traditions of the Egyptian desert, and into its art from Coptic and Syrian sources. It comes out of the wholeness that the Church enjoyed before east and west were torn apart.

This Christianity was forged with a fire and a vigour that spoke as much to the heart as to the head. Out of this crucible came a Christianity full of both tenderness and passion, with a dedication to beauty and yet a commitment to asceticism of the most extreme kind, a triumphant hymning of creation and yet an unswerving devotion to the cross. Here is a Christian understanding which is basic and universal, the primal vision which takes us into the heart of earliest Christendom, and which speaks to that primal vision within all of us. It is something which many people today are looking for but tragically are finding that that search is carrying them outside the structures of the institutional Church.

I had prepared the first draft of this book just before I spent several weeks in Africa. While I was in Johannesburg I decided almost on impulse to spend an evening reading some of these Celtic invocations and prayers, creation credal hymns and hermit nature poems, to a group of people with whom I was spending the week. When I had finished, Mashakane Montjane, a black priest from Soweto, broke into spontaneous applause. "That speaks to the heart," he said, "that touches me deeply, that tells me of things I already know." As I then started to read whatever I could about traditional African spirituality I found extraordinary similarities. For religion both permeated and informed the whole of life, so that there was no formal distinction between the sacred and the secular, the material and the spiritual. In Africa as in Scotland, Ireland and Wales centuries ago, religion accompanied men and women from before birth until after death. It accompanied them in the house and in the fields. Here was a religion which did not call men and women out of their environment, but redeemed them within it.

The price that the Church has paid for its neglect of the Celtic tradition was thus brought home to me very forcibly in Africa. If the nineteenth-century missionaries had been able to speak to the African in these more primal and universal terms that had resonance with what they already knew, perhaps that might have meant a very great difference. But then again, what a difference that might equally well have made in Europe and in North America. The greatest loss undoubtedly has been that of the Celtic understanding of creation. The relationship between people and the land is lost. "The earth no longer speaks man's homely language," the modern Welsh poet Gwenallt tells us. The contemporary concern with green issues and with ecology, and the popularity of the writings of the American Dominican prophet Matthew Fox on creation spirituality, are all evidence of the urgent need to recover and restore what we have neglected and forgotten. But to rediscover something just because we are beginning to see how much we need it again is not the only justification to rekindle the Celtic flame. It is more fundamentally because of its inherent truth, and its inherent beauty, that I believe that the Church, and the world, needs to find again its Celtic roots.

Time and again I have found that I have been brought back to the image of fire and flame. There is that domestic scene of the woman kindling the fire on her hearth at the start of the day. There is the

legend of how St Patrick on Holy Saturday 433 kindled the paschal fire
on the hill of Slane in defiance of the high king Laeghaire of Tara who
sat watching him from the opposite hill of Tara, having decreed that
none should light any fire in the land before he did. As St Patrick and
his followers fled from the wrath of the king they called on God by all
his many names and many powers, and miraculously escaped by being
transformed into deer. The eighth-century "Deer's Cry", more gener-
ally known as St Patrick's breastplate, is one of the greatest of all Celtic
hymns. It sums up much that I have been trying to say. It is a great
litany (and the fact that it obviously owes much to pre-Christian
sources merely adds to its power) which moves from celebration of the
creator God through all the elements in the world of his creating until
finally we are brought down to men and women, each single one of us,
recipient of that protective, all-embracing love. John Taylor quotes it
at the end of one of his books and says that "It sums up and contains all
the spiritual awareness of the primal vision and lifts it into the fullness
of Christ. Would that it were translated and sung in every tongue of
Africa!"[4] And, we might add, in every tongue . . .

I arise today
Through a mighty strength, the invocation of the Trinity,
Through belief in the threeness,
Through confession of the oneness
Of the Creator of Creation.

I arise today
Through the strength of Christ's birth with His baptism,
Through the strength of His crucifixion with His burial,
Through the strength of His resurrection with His ascension,
Through the strength of His coming down for Judgement.

I arise today
Through the strength of the love of Cherubim,
In obedience of angels,

In service of archangels,
In prayers of ancestors,
In predictions of prophets,
In preachings of apostles,
In faith of confessors,
In deeds of righteous men.

I arise today
Through the strength of heaven –
Light of sun,
Radiance of moon,
Splendour of fire,
Speed of lightning,
Swiftness of wind,
Depth of sea,
Stability of earth,
Firmness of rock.

I arise today
Through God's strength to pilot me,
God's might to uphold me,
God's hand to guard me,
God's shield to protect me,
God's host to save me,
From snare of devils,
From temptations of vices,
From all who shall wish me ill,
Afar and anear,
Alone and in multitude.
I summon today all these powers between me and those evils,
Against every cruel merciless power that may oppose my body and
     soul,
Against incantations of false prophets,
Against black laws of paganism,
Against spells of witches,
Against every knowledge that corrupts man's body and soul.

Christ to shield me this day,
So that there come to me abundance of reward.
Christ with me, Christ before me, Christ behind me,
Christ in me, Christ beneath me, Christ above me,
Christ when I lie down, Christ when I sit, Christ when I arise,
Christ in the heart of every man who thinks of me,
Christ in the mouth of everyone who speaks of me,
Christ in every eye that sees me,
Christ in every ear that hears me. [5]

God's World

A woman kneels on the earth floor in her small hut in the Outer Hebrides and lights her fire with this prayer:

> I will kindle my fire this morning
> In the presence of the holy angels of heaven.

She started the day by splashing her face with three palmfuls of water in the name of the Trinity.

> The palmful of the God of Life
> The palmful of the Christ of Love
> The palmful of the Spirit of Peace
>   Triune
>   Of grace.[1]

Then as she makes her bed she had made this a prayerful invocation to the Trinity and a prayerful reflection on the span of life itself.

> I make this bed
>   In the name of the Father, the Son and the Holy Ghost,
>   In the name of the night we were conceived,
>   In the name of the night that we were born,
>   In the name of the day we were baptized,
>   In the name of each night, each day,
>   Each angel that is in the heavens.[2]

And now, at daybreak, before the rest of her family is awake, she starts to do what is her morning chore, to stir into life the fire banked down the night before. Fire was never taken for granted. It was seen as one of the miraculous gifts of God, given so that people have warmth and light, and it was for them at the same time a continual reminder that they too needed constant renewal. The lifting of the peats that brought the flame of the fire to life again was a daily task, done year in, year out. Yet by her words and gestures this woman gives it meaning, for she makes of that first flickering flame a symbol of the love that she keeps burning for herself, her family, the whole family of mankind.

> I will kindle my fire this morning
> In the presence of the holy angels of heaven . . .
> God kindle Thou in my heart within
> A flame of love to my neighbour,
> To my foe, to my friend, to my kindred all . . .
> To the brave, to the knave, to the thrall,
> O son of the loveliest Mary,
> O Son of the loveliest Mary,
> From the lowliest thing that liveth
> To the Name that is highest of all.[3]

The day would end with the "smooring" or smothering of the fire, and again this would be done with a ritual which involved the laying down of the peats in the name of the Trinity and the saints and angels. This was always performed carefully, symbolically, with loving care, the first in the name of the God of life, the second the God of peace, the third the God of grace. Then covering them with ashes, sufficient to subdue but not extinguish the flame, in the name of the Three of Light, she would stretch out her hand and quietly intone a prayer, asking the sacred Three to save and shield and surround her household.

> The sacred Three
> To save
> To shield
> To surround
> The hearth
> The house
> The household
> This eve

This night
And every night
Each single night. Amen.[4]

Saving the fire brings the thought of the saving and protecting grace of Christ, and the saints. This is the common theme which runs through the simple daily prayers and invocations which were collected by Alexander Carmichael and Douglas Hyde in Scotland and Ireland at the end of the last century. The following blessing comes from Ireland but Douglas Hyde in publishing it noted that this kind of prayer might be found "in every place in Ireland and in Scotland also". There are frequently almost exact parallels between the material which they found in the two countries.

As I save this fire tonight
Even so may Christ save me.
On the top of the house let Mary,
Let Bride in its middle be,
Let eight of the mightiest angels
Round the throne of the Trinity
Protect this house and its people
Till the dawn of the day shall be.[5]

Prayers such as these come from people for whom an active living faith was a positive factor in their daily life. There is nothing posed or formal about them. For the men and women who recited them prayer was not a formal exercise; it was a state of mind. Life was lived under the shadow of God's outstretched arm, his protection was constantly sought. They have in them something of the breadth and depth of the psalms. Awe and dread of the might of God and his anger at sin is more than balanced by trust in his love and mercy.[6]

These are the traditional blessings and songs of men and women who had learnt them from their mothers in earliest childhood and who continued to use them for the rest of their lives. They were the prayers of a people who are so busy from dawn to dusk, from dark to dark, that they have little time for long, formal prayers. Instead throughout the day they do whatever has to be done carefully, giving it their full attention, yet at the same time making it the occasion for prayer. Each thing in turn, however humble and mundane it might be, was performed with the help of the Trinity, the saints and the angels. This is totally unselfconscious. It was entirely natural to assume God's presence and partnership from the start of the day until its close. Each of the three persons of the Trinity was acclaimed in turn, for each had an appropriate role to play – quite apart from the fact that saying and doing something rhythmically three times over fitted in so well with much of their daily work.

As the day proceeds whatever has to be done is done with prayer. Before making bread or preparing food women will say, "The luck that God put upon the five loaves and upon the two fishes may He put upon this food."[7] A similar blessing was said at the start of a meal. "The Lord shared the blessing of the five loaves and two fishes with the five thousand. May the blessing of him who gave us this meal be upon us and upon our sharing of this food." This is one version of grace which may be found in all parts of Ireland today. The editor of a collection of traditional Irish prayers, commenting that it is very difficult to do justice to the original metrical form in translation, says that he believes that "we owe this prayer to the influence of monasticism on the lives of the ordinary people, among whom it spread by means of oral tradition".[8] A grace said at the end of the meal runs

A hundred glories to you, bright God of Heavens
Who gave us this food, and the sense to eat it.
Give mercy and glory to our souls
And life without sin to ourselves and to the poor.[9]

The milking blessings probably more than any others reveal the extent to which the women felt themselves at home with Christ and the saints, who they know are standing beside them ready to give practical help and support. So as they milk they turn to them:

Come, Mary, and milk my cow,
Come, Bride, and encompass her,
Come, Columba the benign,
And twine thine arm around my cow.

Come, Mary Virgin, to my cow,
Come, great Bride, the beauteous,
Come, thou milkmaid of Jesus Christ
And place thine arms beneath my cow.[10]

They pray not only for their own hands but also for the teats of the cow.

Bless O God my little cow
Bless O God my desire;
Bless Thou my partnership
And the milking of my hands, O God.

Bless O God each teat
Bless O God each finger;
Bless Thou each drop
That goes into my pitcher, O God.[11]

Milking is followed by making butter, and as she churns the woman will think of the apostles whom she can see standing outside her window, waiting impatiently with Mary and Jesus for a buttered bannock. She takes pride in the quality of her work, and wants to do the very best possible since it is for Jesus himself and the saints.

Come, thou Brigit, handmaid calm;
Hasten the butter on the cream;
Seest thou impatient Peter yonder
Waiting the buttered bannock white and yellow.

Stillim! steolim!
Strichim! streoichim!
Send down the broken
And bring up the whole!

> Come, thou Mary Mother mild,
> Hasten the butter on the cream;
> Seest thou Paul and John and Jesus
> Waiting the gracious butter yonder.
>
> Stillim! steolim!
> Strichim! streoichim!
> Send down the broken
> And bring up the whole![12]

It would seem entirely natural to turn to St Brigit and ask for her help with the dairy since these domestic matters were always particularly associated with her. They might remember how she herself had asked for a blessing on her own kitchen.

> Mary's Son, my Friend, cometh
> To bless my kitchen . . .
> My kitchen,
> The kitchen of the white God,
> A kitchen which my King hath blessed,
> A kitchen that hath butter.[13]

It was said of St Brigit that in her mountain dairy she divided her churning into twelve in honour of the apostles, and the thirteenth in honour of Christ, greater than the others and kept to be given to the poor and to guests. Hospitality has always been important. An old Kerry woman in the south-west of Ireland today still recites a poem which may well be in origin as old as the tenth or eleventh century.

> I would like to have the men of Heaven
> In my own house;
> With vats of good cheer
> Laid out for them.
>
> I would like to have the three Marys,
> Their fame is so great.
> I would like people
> From every corner of Heaven.

I would like them to be cheerful
In their drinking,
I would like to have Jesus too
Here amongst them.

I would like a great lake of beer
For the King of Kings,
I would like to be watching Heaven's family
Drinking it through all eternity.[14]

The work of the household, whether churning, grinding corn or making cloth, particularly when these were communal activities, was associated with many traditional rituals. The invocation of the Trinity of course went naturally with any action that was done three times. Thus if women were "waulking" the cloth, that is stretching it on a frame to strengthen and thicken it, one of them, who was the consecrator or celebrant, would at sunrise place the roll of cloth in the centre of the frame, turn it slowly and name each member of the household for whom it was intended:

This is not cloth for priest or cleric
But it is cloth for my own little Donald of love,
For my companion beloved, for John of joy,
And for Muriel of loveliest hue.

Then the cloth was spat upon and slowly reversed in the name of the Father, Son and Spirit. In this way every woof and warp and every thread was consecrated to God. At the same time it was assumed that he himself was there, placing his arm around each woman as she waulked.

Place Thou thine arm around
Each woman who shall be waulking it,
And do Thou aid her in the hour
Of her need.[15]

Weaving and the loom, grinding and the quern, making butter and the churn – whatever the activity both action and instrument were committed to God for his protection and blessing. "Consecrate the four posts of my loom." "Give Thy blessing everywhere, on every shuttle passing under the thread." "Hasten the butter on the cream." Tools and activities are held up to God with complete honesty. Nothing could be less sentimental; or more down to earth. These prayers are totally specific, addressed to a God who is seen to be involved in daily reality, not excluded from it.

The men's days spent on the farms, the fields or at sea, fishing or herding, sowing and reaping, inevitably involved time walking between home and the place of work. Whatever the distance they would never set out on any journey without first asking a blessing, however simple.

I on Thy path O God
Thou God in my steps.

Bless to me, O God
The earth beneath my foot,
Bless to me, O God,
The path whereon I go.[16]

A journey becomes a time for them to walk with God and for God to walk with them. They assume his companionship on the road, a companionship of such ease and familiarity that they actually laugh as they go because of the certainty of the presence of the Trinity beside them.

My walk this day with God,
My walk this day with Christ,
My walk this day with Spirit.
The threefold all-kindly:
Ho! ho! ho! the Threefold all-kindly.

My shielding this day from ill,
My shielding this night from harm,
Ho! ho! both my soul and my body,

Be by Father, by Son, by Holy Spirit:
By Father, by Son, by Holy Spirit.

Be the Father shielding me,
Be the Son shielding me,
Be the Spirit shielding me,
As Three and as One:
Ho! ho! ho! as Three and as One.[17]

As they led their animals to the pastures they knew that they could trust the King of all shepherds to look after them well since he might be assumed to have some practical experience in the matter. When a man left his flocks at the pasture in the morning he would take leave of them tenderly, waving a blessing over them in complete confidence that for the rest of the day they would be in the safe hands of God and the saints.

The herding of Bride to the kine
Whole and well may you return.

The prosperity of Mary Mother be yours
Active and full may you return.

The safeguard of Columba round your feet,
Whole be your return home.

By the bright Michael King of the angels
Protecting, keeping, and saving you.

The guarding of God and the Lord be yours
Till I or mine shall see you again.

The herding of fair Mary
Be about your head, your body, and aiding you.[18]

Another herding blessing asked for safekeeping:

Closed to you be every pit
Smooth to you be every hill,
Snug to you be every bare spot,
Beside the cold mountains.

The sanctuary of Mary Mother be yours . . .
The protection of shapely Cormac be yours . . .
The fellowship of Mary Mother be yours,
The fellowship of Brigit of kine be yours,
The fellowship of Michael victorious be yours,
In nibbling, in chewing, in munching.[19]

Tradition and ritual were important in the changing pattern of the farming year. Many ceremonies seem to incorporate earlier pre-Christian elements while at the same time asking for the blessing of the Trinity. Seed-corn had to be prepared for three days before it was sown. A man would walk around it in the direction of the sun, sprinkling it with clear, cold water in the name of the Trinity, so that the sowing itself could begin on a Friday, a day held to be auspicious for any activity except one that involved the use of iron, since that reminded them of the nails used in the Crucifixion. When the corn was ripe enough to be cut the whole family dressed in their best, and the father would take up his sickle and face the sun, and cutting a handful of corn would put it sunwise three times round his head in a reaping salutation which the others then followed.

God, bless Thou thyself my reaping,
Each ridge, and plain, and field,
Each sickle curved, shapely, hard,
Each ear and handful in the sheaf;
Each ear and handful in the sheaf.[20]

There were blessings for the changing rhythm not only of each day and each succeeding year but also blessings to mark the cycle of birth and death in every human life. From the very first moment of its life, when at birth a mother commended her baby to the Trinity, ritual and rhythm would play an important role. The new-born infant would be handed across the fire three times, and then carried sunwise three times round the hearth before the mother, with the help of her neighbours who had assisted at the birth, placed three drops of water on its forehead. "And I beseech the Holy Three to lave and to bathe the child and to preserve it to Themselves. All the people in the house are raising their voices with the watching-women, giving witness that the child has been committed to the blessed Trinity." This took place in the home and was the mother's baptism preceding the formal, "clerical" baptism eight days later when the child was formally received into the Church. The ceremony in the house with family and neighbours was, as one woman in the Outer Hebrides told Alexander Carmichael, full of meaning: "By the Book itself ear has never heard music more beautiful than the music of the watching-women when they are consecrating the seed of man and committing him to the great God of life."[21]

In the name of God,
In the name of Jesus,
In the name of Spirit,
The perfect Three of power.

The little drop of the Father
On thy little forehead, beloved one.

The little drop of the Son
On thy little forehead, beloved one.

The little drop of the Spirit
On thy little forehead, beloved one.

To aid thee, to guard thee,
To shield thee, to surround thee.

To keep thee from the fays,
To shield thee from the host.

To sain thee from the gnome,
To deliver thee from the spectre.

The little drop of the Three
To shield thee from the sorrow.

The little drop of the Three
To fill thee with Their pleasantness.

The little drop of the Three
To fill thee with Their virtue.

O the little drop of the Three
To fill thee with Their virtue.[22]

When the time came for the sons and daughters to leave home the mother would give them a parting blessing, and again commit them to the care and protection of the Trinity.

The benison of God be to thee,
The benison of Christ be to thee,
The benison of Spirit be to thee,
And to thy children,
To thee and to thy children.

The peace of God be to thee,
The peace of Christ be to thee,
The peace of Spirit be to thee,
During all thy life,
All the days of thy life.

The keeping of God upon thee in every pass,
The shielding of Christ upon thee in every path,
The bathing of Spirit upon thee in every stream,
In every land and sea thou goest.[23]

Life itself will end, as each day as ended, with a bed-blessing.

> I lie in my bed
> As I would lie in the grave.

Perhaps nothing speaks as tenderly and securely of what the presence of the Trinity can mean than a bed-blessing such as this:

> I am lying down tonight as beseems
> In the fellowship of Christ, son of the Virgin of ringlets,
> In the fellowship of the gracious Father of glory,
> In the fellowship of the Spirit of powerful aid.
>
> I am lying down tonight with God,
> And God tonight will lie down with me,
> I will not lie down tonight with sin, nor shall
> Sin or sin's shadow lie down with me.
>
> I am lying down tonight with the Holy Spirit,
> And the Holy Spirit this night will lie down with me,
> I will lie down this night with the Three of my love,
> And the Three of my love will lie down with me.[24]

An Irish blessing runs:

> I lay me down with Thee, O Jesus
> And mayest Thou be about my bed,
> The oil of Christ be upon my soul,
> The Apostles' Creed be above my head.
> O Father who wrought me
> O Son who bought me
> O Spirit who sought me
> Let me be Thine.[25]

Birth and death, waking and sleeping, and in between all the working hours of each day, are all part of a life in which the presence of God is known. Living and praying are inseparable. Much of that praying, with its frequent repetition, was of a rhythmical nature that responded well to the actual work itself. And here again the Celtic touches something that is universal to us all, even if in our sophisticated world today we far too often tend to forget it. These work-songs and blessings engage with something which is basic, fundamental; they go back to something which the earlier bards and minstrels knew: the close connection between music and religion. Both have at their heart rhythm. To move with this is to be in tune, literally, with one's self and the world; to lose it is to get cross-grained, to find alienation and disharmony.

Praying is not separated from singing or working or any other aspect of life. Because of the way in which they saw their world they were ready to accept, enjoy, transform whatever lay at hand. The pattern of the day, of the year, and of the whole of life itself, was lived out totally in the presence of God and the saints. Every moment of the day, every activity becomes a way to God. There was nothing self-conscious about this; rather, it seemed entirely natural. It meant, in the words of a young Irish farm-servant at the end of the last century, laying "our caring and our keeping and our saving on the Sacred Trinity."[26] Life was lived at two levels – the practical tasks of daily life are done for their own sake carefully and competently, but simultaneously they become signs of God's all-encompassing love. A thing is done well not only for itself but because of the part that that plays in God's world. It matters that the butter is made well or that the herds are driven carefully since God himself is involved. He cares about the things of his world. Work is, after all, a matter of partnership with him, something through which he may be better known. Celtic spirituality is deeply incarnational. It is through his world, in its totality, however mundane and down to earth, that God reveals himself. So the Celtic way of seeing the world is infused with the sense of the all-pervading presence of God. This is God's world, a world to be claimed, affirmed and honoured.

the

dedicated life

Monks and Hermits

"I ought not to conceal God's gift which he lavished on me in the land of my captivity, because then I sought him earnestly and I found him there, and he protected me from all evils, as I believe, because of his spirit dwelling in me, which has been at work within me up to the present day." Almost at the start of his Confession St Patrick breaks into this great hymn of praise to the God who brought him back to Ireland and blessed his work there. The next paragraph moves into a tremendous credal affirmation, celebrating the creation, and the power of the Trinity. [1] St Patrick himself had first been brought to Ireland as a slave at the age of sixteen, and for six years afterwards served his master as a shepherd. These were years spent in the solitude and wilderness of the mountains and they had become for him a time of prayer. "I would say up to a hundred prayers in one day and almost as many at night: I would even stay in the forests and on the mountain, and would wake to pray before dawn in all weathers, snow, frost, rain." This man who celebrates the Trinitarian God, and who finds it natural to pray out of doors as he herds the sheep, is the man to whom traditionally Ireland owes its Christianity. Already we can see here something of its peculiar genius.

The actual historical foundations remain however much more difficult to establish with any sort of certainty. Even though the greatness of St Patrick cannot be disputed it seems much more likely that the diffusion of Christianity in Ireland took place rather more gradually, beginning perhaps a century or so before his mission in the middle years of the fifth century (precise dates are disputed), and taking a further two centuries to complete. The sequence of events is not perhaps of such great importance. The characteristics of the Church which emerged during these years, and above all the very particular development of the monasticism which shaped it, are the subject of this chapter for it is this which laid the foundation for Celtic Christianity.

In a letter which St Columbanus wrote to the Pope in the sixth century he described the Irish as a people "living on the edge of the world". It was a proud boast. It is also a significant clue if we are to appreciate the development of the Church in Ireland. The geographical location of the country, on the very western edge of Europe, explains why Christianity reached the country so late. This brought with it certain important consequences. Rome had never penetrated as far as here, and as a result there was none of the imperial infrastructure, found elsewhere in Europe, on which to build the Church. Instead there was a land with a strong, indigenous society and culture, a heroic, tribal society, with a long tradition of native learning. Much of this was to be absorbed and taken up, and was to colour the way in which Christianity was received and diffused. The Irish Church never turned its back on its past but rather rejoiced in its secular and pagan traditions. Here life was rural, hierarchical, family-based. Towns were non-existent; there was no tradition of urban life or culture. The chief landowners each lived in their own ring fort, the rath, as a small self-contained community, and formed part of a tribal area. Kingship was strong, and a king ruled his own tuath or tribe with a high-king over him who claimed sovereignty of the whole of Ireland. This kind of grouping was naturally carried over into the Church. There was little to differentiate an early monastery from a fortified homestead, except that in addition to its encircling wall and its number of small, rough huts inside, there would also be a church. These foundations, the centres from which the pastoral work of the Church radiated, were founded by certain great families, and it was the custom to choose the abbot or head of the monastery from the founder's family. Each monastery was independent, but it might exercise control over a number of daughter-houses, scattered, smaller foundations, so that the abbot was responsible for their jurisdiction as well. Each had its own rule or "code of behaviour".

As a result it was not long before Ireland was covered with a number of great monastic houses, together with the lesser settlements attached to them. The Latin system of territorial, diocesan organization never came into being here. In less than a hundred years after the coming of

St Patrick the Church in Ireland was not diocesan but monastic, governed by the abbots of important monasteries who might themselves be bishops or who might include a bishop among the members of their community.

Nowhere else in Christendom was the culture of a people so completely embraced within monasticism.[2] St Patrick himself tells us how astonished he was at the numbers of his newly baptized who chose to be monks and virgins of Christ. The same was also true in Wales. One of the reasons was that monasticism fitted so easily into the existing pattern of society. A monastery represented the religious activity of the tribe, it could only be founded in accordance with tribal land law, and so close were the tribal connections that if necessary a layman could be the abbot rather than allow it to be ruled by an alien monk.[3] The abbot took on a patriarchal role, maintaining his influence and power at the expense of the prestige of the episcopate. An amusing sidelight on this is the fact that while in Anglo-Saxon law a bishop had the status of an earldorman, the principal administrator of the shire, in Welsh law his standing was no more than that of a free tribesman. The leadership of the Church thus lay in the hands of the monks. The monastic emphasis was so strong that the Pope was known as "Abbot of Rome" and Christ himself would sometimes be called "the Abbot of the Blessed in Heaven".

When a suitable site for a monastery had been established and time had been spent in fasting and prayer, the founder would mark out the boundaries of his settlement, or rath, and start to work to build the ditch and the enclosing wall. Modelled on the ring fort, the appearance of the monastic community would thus be that of a scattered cluster of small buildings encircled by a protective earthen wall. This wall however was neither fortification nor traditional enclosure for there was always much coming and going. The community was large and varied, with probably a big population of lay tenants. Most buildings were very simple, of wood or wattle and daub, with the church alone in stone. Even this was extremely small and unpretentious, without any attempt at architectural distinction. If the community grew larger it was usual to build more small churches rather than enlarge the main one. The monks themselves would usually be two or three to a cell. Separate cells might be allowed as a special privilege to older men in their declining years. The abbot at Iona had a hut to himself and this may have been the general custom. Special cells would also have been available for the artists, for all those engaged in the work of book-making, as well as for the craftsmen who were needed to make bells, vestments or crosses.

When from about the tenth century the great bell towers were built their actual physical appearance must have made a striking statement about the power of monasticism in the land. Sixty-five are still to be seen today in Ireland; tall and slender they range in height from 70 to 120 feet, and taper gracefully towards the distinctive bell cap. They always stand a short distance from the church and community which they overshadow, and even though they could become places of refuge, their main function was to provide a high place from which the hand bell, to call people to prayer, could be rung. These were four-sided iron or bronze bells, tall and narrow, formed of plates of metal that were bent into shape and riveted, and struck from such a great height their sound could travel in all directions.

> Sweet little bell
> That is rung on a windy night.[4]

With their offices and workshops, cells and oratories, rooms for lay people and guests these great monasteries brought numbers of people together, a wide and varied community, with many differing vocations and occupations gathered into a place where they could all in some way or other share the same values and deepen the quality of life.

Why did people go into monasteries in the early Celtic Church? There were of course a number of sociological reasons since by so integrating itself into local society the monastery was landlord, a patron of the arts, dispenser of alms and hospitality. But beyond all this there was simply the search for God. There is no complete philosophy of the monastic life in the early records, but whether the sermons attributed to St Columbanus are really by him or not they certainly give us the fullest early statement of monastic ideals.[5]

"Taste and see", he says "how lovely, how pleasant is the Lord." The monastery is the place in which to practise contemplation and the life of prayer that will lead men and women to Christ. "May no one and nothing separate us from the love of Christ . . . that we may abide in him here and for ever." And again, "Live in Christ that Christ may live in you." This asks considerable commitment, for the true disciple must be in the same state as Christ, renouncing worldly goods, "satisfied with the small possessions of utter need". Until there is an asceticism by which the monk strips himself of self he will never reach "the most perfect and perpetual love of God". There can be no doubt about the demands. The monk must be ready to do battle with all the forces that constantly assail him. But the presence of God is not simply something to be longed for and worked for, the heavenly goal which is the reward of the battle and the discipline. It is also attainable here and to be enjoyed now. "God is near," this is the message; God is close at hand. "From the hour I set my mind on God I never took it away from him," said St Brigit. For St Ide Christ comes in the form of a baby at her breast, the closest possible of any relationship. A ninth-century poem tells of her wish. "I will take nothing from my Lord", said she, "unless He gives me His Son from Heaven in the form of a baby to be nursed by me . . . So that Christ came to her in the form of a baby, and she said then:

"Little Jesus, who is nursed by me in my little hermitage – even a priest with store of wealth, all is false but little Jesus.

"It is Jesus, noble and angelic, not a paltry priest, Who is nursed by me in my little hermitage; Jesus the son of the Jewess."[6]

Another extremely important role which the monasteries played in local life was that of centres of learning and culture. It seems highly probable that this owed much to their connections with those well-developed colleges of pre-Christian Ireland in which druids and bards underwent their courses of instruction. For the highest degree in attainment of learning a twelve-year period of disciplined study was needed in the druidic school, for the standards were demanding. With the coming of Christianity the monks took over some of these functions. Possibly almost as important was the knowledge which they gained by listening to native learning, to poetry and stories of magic and healing. That this heroic literature, preserved through oral tradition, was known to the monks, seems clear from evidence in the seventh century of a corpus of native heathen lore and literature which was transcribed in the little monastery of Drumsnat in county Monaghan.[7] A twelfth-century satire has a delightful picture of a hermit who comes out of his cell with his boots stuffed with heroic tales.[8] Even when the druids disappeared the bards remained numerous and influential. St Columba seems to have found it quite natural to go and find the bard Gemman and stay with him for a time in Leinster. The Irish church owed much to its pre-Christian past for it never repudiated its earlier cultural heritage, and this is reflected not only in its love for study, but also in its retention of many literary forms such as the lorica prayers.

But Ireland also received a Christianity and a monasticism which preserved very many Eastern elements, and it kept this Eastern emphasis while horizons in the rest of Europe were growing narrower. While it is possible to try to establish the direct links and influences, it also seems that in some indefinable way the heroic-age Celtic spirit was naturally predisposed to find something sympathetic in the stark asceticism and the extremism of the ideals of the Egyptian desert. The number of times that St Antony of Egypt and St Paul of Thebes are shown in the high crosses is not without significance. Many monastic texts of this early period commend these two saints as models. The monks of Brittany looked upon them as the first teachers of a life of solitary rigour.[9] The Stowe missal, the only surviving mass book of the Irish church, written at Tallaght in the early ninth century, includes their names, together with other anchorites of the desert of Scete in lower Egypt.[10] And the Life of Columcille in the Book of Lismore listing three ways in which men are summoned to knowledge of God and membership of his family puts first "the urging and kindling of men by the divine grace to serve the Lord after the manner of Paul, and of Antony the monk, and of the other faithful monks who used to serve God there in Egypt."[11]

The revival of trade between Ireland and the East, and the communications which were opened up by both land and sea, brought travellers, artists, monks and scholars in its train. Ships from Alexandria or Constantinople would come to southern Spain, sail up to Seville and then continue into the Atlantic and so to Ireland. Recent research shows the extent of that influence in so many different areas of life, whether the Coptic influence on the illuminations of the Book of

Kells, or the influence of the Mozarabic liturgy on Irish liturgical books. The study of Greek within the Irish monasteries may have been rudimentary but when Greek died out in the rest of Europe the Irish still had a smattering of the language. The way in which the Irish approached the psalter differed in certain significant ways from the rest of Europe, and finds parallels with fourth-century Edessa or Antioch.[12] Seven monks from Egypt who died while visiting Ireland and were buried there are mentioned in a litany in the book of Leinster.[13] A carving on the cross of Moone showing two cichlids, Egyptian mouth-breeding fish, to illustrate the loaves and the fishes in the parable of the feeding of the five thousand, remains one of the most unexpected, as also one of the most delightful, examples of this eastern influence.[14]

Sixth-century Ireland has been described by Nora Chadwick as "the outermost ripple of the great monastic movement of the Greek and Coptic churches of the East".[15] Here was a Christianity in which there was no room for mediocrity.[16] The anchorites, or hermits, who were such a distinctive feature of the whole Celtic Church almost from its earliest days, are an example of its marked asceticism. From at least the sixth century anchorites played an important part within the monastic movement, associated with all the great monastic foundations. In most cases the hermit life was regarded as such a serious undertaking that it was only to be embarked upon after many years in the community and with the approval of the abbot. In the "Rule of the Anchorites" ascribed to St Columba it is made clear that the hermit is to be apart in a desert place, in the neighbourhood of a chief monastery. There are many dramatic accounts of what was involved in this life. It was the desert of Egypt translated into lonely and isolated places in the depths of Ireland, Scotland or Wales – places that still today bear the names Disserth or Dysart. Here in a clearing in thickly wooded countryside, or on a rocky promontory on the coast, or perhaps on one of the island fastnesses, men would dedicate themselves to lives of prayer, in silence and solitude. Skellig Michael, lying twelve miles off the southwest tip of the Kerry coast, must be one of the most dramatic sites, "the most westerly of Christ's fortresses in the Western world". Hermits who chose to settle on islands such as this were likely to be subjecting themselves to long periods of more or less total isolation. Those on the islands off the west coast of Scotland, or far out to sea in the Atlantic, were choosing to live in places made largely inaccessible for much of the year. The island of Bardsey, off the Lleyn peninsula in north Wales, known as "the burial place of twenty thousand saints", has become again today a place of pilgrimage – but one which still remains inaccessible for several months each winter.

Yet this isolation was of course what these earliest hermits sought. "There is no retreat in the world such as this space which I am now destined to inhabit," said St Gwynllyw as he found the situation he sought on the banks of a river in the depths of Wales. "Happy therefore is the place, happier is he who inhabits it."[17] These solitary places were to become their "place of resurrection". The phrase that occurs time and again in the lives of the saints tells us much of the underlying vision which sustained them as they undertook lives of almost unbelievable hardship. St Kevin after he had settled at Glendalough ate only "nuts of the wood and plants of the ground and pure water to drink; and he had no bed but a pillow of stone and a flag on each side of him, and he had no dwelling above him, and the skins of wild beasts were clothing for him."[18]

The lives of the saints, which must of course not be taken as literal accounts but rather as rich compilations of traditional legend and hagiography, give many impressive accounts of these austerities, the austerity of the site itself increased by their own self-inflicted austerities. St Maedoc "the marvellous of the mighty deeds was seven full years fasting in Drumlane, without milk or ale, without flesh or kitchen, but only a little bit of barley bread and a little drink of milk every third Sunday, lying on the bare ground or a stone full hard, without any covering or clothing except the skins of wild, untamed animals, continually reciting his psalms and psalters, and praying zealously to God; for he used to recite thrice fifty psalms every day on cold clammy stones . . ."[19] Of St Illtud it was told that he watched and fasted assiduously and prayed without ceasing, and that "in the middle of the night before mattins he used to wash himself in cold water and to remain in it as long as the Lord's prayer could be said three times."[20] The tales of endurance could be multiplied time after time. This isolation however was modified by the friendships which the hermits established with the birds and animals around them. The natural creatures of the forests and the seas kept them company and helped them with their daily needs. The stories of their shared life will be considered more fully later; they tell us a great deal about the Celtic understanding of common creation.[21]

But the Celtic eremitical tradition was modified in another direction. There was here no idea that the hermit life was an absolute, an alternative to the coenobetic life in community. There was rather a flexibility, a recognition of the interconnectedness between the two. This meant that monks might retire into solitude at some times in their lives, or perhaps at certain times in the year, and then later on re-emerge to join in a more active life. So the hermit ideal is not an alternative to the apostolic life, but both are seen as having complementary roles to play. Great apostles and missionaries like St Columbanus or St Columba are recorded as seeking out and retiring to solitary spots as part of the pattern of their public activities. The contemplative life and pastoral concerns go hand in hand. "You know that I love the salvation of many, and seclusion for myself; the one for the progress of the Lord, that is, of His Church; the other for my own desire."[22] St Columbanus spent much of his time organizing his monastic foundations in Burgundy and in preaching missions. Yet he used to withdraw regularly to a cave (from which he had turned out a bear), particularly on the vigils of feast days, for solitary prayer, sometimes withdrawing for long periods at a stretch, sometimes being there for fifty days or more. Fursey, after preaching for ten years in Ireland "unable to stand the crowds overwhelming him", retreated with a few brothers to an island, but then later left for East Anglia where he founded a monastery, until "desiring to separate himself from every care of the world" he finally withdrew to Gaul, so that the pattern of his life was of lengthy successive periods of pastoral work, followed by seclusion, repeated two or three times. Mo-Chuta, having sought out a cave on the banks of the river Blackwater to escape the noise of the new foundation at Lismore, begun in 638, spent eighteen months there, but when he felt death approaching had himself carried back to the monastery.[23] In another instance the hermit life laid the foundation for the subsequent apostolic life. St Paulin at the age of eighteen wanted to live as a hermit "after the example of the glorious father Antony, who first taught the servants of Christ to seek lonely places of retreat in the wilderness". He spent time at Llandensant in Carmarthenshire, a place of great solitude, austerity and beauty, in reading, fasting, and prayer. But when he was summoned by King Marc of Cornwall to leave this in order that he might come and instruct the King and his people, he turned from the contemplative to the active life. After some years however, "on fire with the longing for perfection the idea occurred to him of leaving the land of his fathers and crossing the sea to foreign lands where he might live unknown to all save to God alone", he went to a hermitage in Brittany where "by prayer, fasting, meditation on the divine scriptures, constant vigils, practising humility, patience and cleanness of heart and body, he became a torch illuminating the dark places of Brittany". Before his death around the year 580 he was consecrated "despite his unwillingness and tears".[24]

Steep Holm, Flat Holm and Barry, three islands in the Bristol Channel, were often inhabited by solitaries, not always as permanent abodes but for periods of seclusion between missionary journeys or during Lent. So the active and the contemplative were held in tension. The balance of activity within the world and retirement from it is well caught in the ninth-century life of St Declan. "For he was in his own dear cell which he had built for himself. It is between the wood and the sea in a narrow secret place above the ocean-edge. A clear stream of water flows from the hill into the sea and trees encircle it beautifully. It is called Declan's disert and lies a short mile away from the (monastic city). Thither the holy bishop Declan used to withdraw to rest alone with God in fasting and vigil . . . He dearly loved his little cell in which he could, for short periods, be alone with God."[25] The solitary life was in fact practised in the Celtic tradition with a variety of observance and a flexibility of structure, some hermits almost totally isolated, some living in a hermitage attached to a monastery, others seasonal hermits who from time to time found a space for "a season of solitude".

Each individual, as indeed each monastic community, went its own way. Celtic monasticism carried no stereotype. A rich variety of people chose to live out the monastic life. There was no expectation that any particular Rule would set out to produce a particular kind of person, other than a saint. Eight monastic Rules have come down to us from the ancient Irish Church, six written in poetry and two in prose. The four which date from the early period before the year 800 emphasize the virtues of the Gospel and could be a rule of life for any Christian. Only later do we find any detailed reference to the ordering of life in community. The Rule of St Comgall, founder of the monastery at Bangor, who died in 602 opens

> Preserve the rule of the Lord;
> in this way you will run no risk;
> Try not to transgress it
> as long as your life lasts.

> This is the most important part of the rule;
> love Christ; hate wealth;
> Devotion to the king of the sun
> and kindness to people.

These early rules emphasize the values of the Gospel, the love of Christ, the living out of a virtuous life. Much was written in the form of simple injunctions. "Remain very close to Christ." "Do not aim at ostentatious holiness." "Do not be hard and miserly." The need for love, patience and humility are common themes.

> These are your three rules –
> do not hold anything dearer –
> patience, humility and
> love of the Lord in your heart.

Inevitably there is a great deal about penitence and repentance. This is taken from The Rule of Comgall.

> Repentance is sluggishness
> after being in great sin
> will have small reward in heaven
> and its trial by fire will be great.

> If anybody enters the path of repentance
> it is sufficient
> to advance a step every day.
> Do not wish to be like a charioteer.

If you practise repentance,
if your heart is meek,
your way will be straight
to the king of the kingdom of heaven.

The importance of accepting the guidance of a wise and holy man
was also set out clearly.

Though you may think you are very solid
it is not good to be your own guide.

The art of *anamchairdeas* or soul-friendship was of peculiar importance.
The rule of St Carthage, who founded the famous monastery of Lismore
in Co. Waterford, probably written about two hundred years after the
founder's death in 636, addresses a whole section of the Rule to the
duties of the soul-friend who deals with penitents.

If you be anybody's soul-friend,
do not sell his soul.
Do not be a blind man leading the blind.
Do not allow him to fall into neglect.

There is a traditional story of a discussion between the heads of two
monasteries about the virtues of abstinence or not, to which the reply
was that neither should claim superiority since everyone would get to
heaven in any case. Each monastery went its own way. The antiphon-
ary of Bangor, the oldest surviving liturgical book of the Celtic Church,
contains a poem written by a monk of the monastery which allows us to
see what this way of life has meant to him.

Good the Rule of Bangor
correct and divine.
Strict, holy, constant,
Exalted, just and admirable.

Blessed the company of Bangor
founded on certain faith.
Graced with the hope of salvation,
Perfect in love.

Surely an enduring city
Strong and united . . .
The fold also of Christ's flock
kept by the Supreme Father.

The Rule attributed to St Carthage expresses this sense of individuality very nicely.

We watch, we read, we pray,
Each according to his strength . . .

Without the vow of stability (as still in the East today) some of the Rules ask the abbot to be moderate so that nobody may have cause to leave the house because the yoke is too heavy. The abbot is to be like Christ in the Gospel. Some of the most moving lines in these Rules are those which speak of gentleness and non-violence and forgiveness.

To forgive every one
who has done us evil,
in voice, in word, in deed,
is the command of the king of heaven.

to love those who hate us
in this earthly world;
to do good to those who persecute us
is the command of God.[26]

Hospitality was always important. The monk may entertain guests, just as the monk in his individual cell in Egypt. The rule of Ailbe, written in 750, says

A clean house for the guests
and a big fire,
washing and bathing for them,
and a couch without sorrow

Yet undoubtedly the life was a hard one. The hours of prayer were long; the saying of the psalms a relentless demand. The image of the anvil used in one rule catches something of the perseverance and tenacity which the life asked of its followers.

the battle against many vices;
the battle against body;
the battle against the devil.

But ultimately there was the promise of the Kingdom of Heaven, and the welcome from the God who the monks see as an abbot, "the abbot of the archangels" who, as the Rule of Emly put it, will say "come here and welcome".

Any account of Celtic monasticism must become an account far more of persons than of institutions. It revolves around the achievements of men and women who have become known to us for the dedication of their lives. To their contemporaries they were soon known as saints. Their lives of single-minded devotion have given rise to many legends which have become so marked a characteristic of Celtic Christianity. In them we encounter people of whom very often almost humanly impossible things are related. They see visions, talk with angels, repulse demons, stop rivers in their courses, raise the dead, tame fierce beasts. The supernatural is always breaking in. They are men of power. Miracles are recounted as though they are the most natural of daily occurrences.

Much of this demands in us today a suspension of our rational judgement. It is only too easy to be sceptical. Yet by dismissing too lightly we become losers. Legends of the saints endure because we all need holy people. The saints are heroes, symbols of what could be possible; a reminder that everything cannot be reduced to manageable, cerebral categories, and that there is a dimension beyond what our logical minds dictate. So the stories of their lives and miracles persist. Men and women "loaned by eternity to guide this present life", is no bad epitaph for them. The saints are the heroes of a new order, as splendid as were their earlier pre-Christian forerunners. Most of them are not of course saints by canonization; they are men and women honoured by their own contemporaries for the holiness of their lives of self-denial and self- discipline. Stories grow up around them because they represent an ideal which is for most people unattainable; they become symbols of what is, or what could be, possible. Holiness always remains compelling.

St Columba, one of the most familiar and well-loved of all Celtic monks, has the advantage of a very distinguished biographer in Adomnan who wrote his life a comparatively short time after his death. Here we are shown both the humanity of the man and also those qualities of holiness which his contemporaries recognized, and which in their eyes carried him beyond the limitations of the present world. The pages which tell of his last day on earth sum up much that has been said here about monastic holiness. As we follow those last hours we see the man himself, in all his gentleness, the love he commands not only from the brothers but also from the animals. We see his dedication to the life of prayer and that golden light which infused the oratory as he enters it for the last time speaks vividly of how the heavenly was never far away.

"Truly this day is for me a Sabbath, because it is my last day of this present laborious life." As he sat at rest beside a cross by the roadside, St Columba himself was well aware that this was his last day on earth. Adomnan, the faithful scribe, gives his detailed account of how that day unfolded. "Behold, a white horse came to him, the obedient servant who was accustomed to carry the milk-vessels between the cow-pasture and the monastery. It went to the saint, and strange to tell put its head in his bosom, inspired, as I believe, by God, before whom every living creature has understanding, with such perception of things as the Creator himself has decreed; and knowing that its master would presently depart from it, and that it should see him no more, it began to mourn, and like a human being to let tears fall freely on the lap of the saint, and foaming much, to weep aloud. When he saw this, the attendant began to drive away the weeping mourner; but the saint forbade him, saying: 'Let him, let him that loves us, pour out the tears of most bitter grief here in my bosom. See, a man though you are, and having a rational soul you could by no means know anything of my departure except what I myself have even now disclosed to you. But to this brute and unreasoning animal the Creator has, in what way he would, revealed clearly that its master is going to depart from it.' Thus speaking, he blessed his servant the horse, as it turned sadly away from him.

"Going from there, he climbed a small hill overlooking the monastery, and stood on its summit for a little while. And as he stood he raised both hands, and blessed his monastery, saying: 'Oh this place, small and mean though it be, not only the kings of the Irish with their peoples, but also the rulers of barbarous and foreign nations, with their subjects, will bestow great and especial honour; also special reverence will be bestowed by saints even of other churches.'

"After these words he descended from that little hill, returned to the monastery, and sat in the hut, writing a psalter. And when he came to that verse of the thirty-third Psalm where it is written, 'But they that seek the Lord shall not want for anything that is good', he said: 'Here, at the end of the page, I must stop. Let Baithene write what follows.' . . . He then entered the church for vespers and at its close returned to his lodging, and reclining on his sleeping-place, the bare rock for his bed and a stone for his pillow, he spoke for the last time to the brethren. When he stopped speaking he was silent for a little while.

"Then, when the beaten bell resounded at midnight, he rose in haste and went to the church and running, entered in advance of the others, alone; and bowing his knees in prayer he sank down beside the altar. In that moment Diormit, the attendant, following later, saw from a distance the whole church filled inside with angelic light about the saint. As Diormit approached the doorway, the light that he had seen quickly faded. A few more of the brothers also had seen it, when they too were a little way off.

"So Diormit entering the church cried in a tearful voice: 'Where are you, where are you, father?' And groping in the darkness, since the lamps of the brothers had not yet been brought, he found the saint lying before the altar. Raising him a little, and sitting down beside him, he placed the holy head upon his lap. Meanwhile the company of monks ran up with lights; and when they saw that their father was dying they began to lament. And as we have learned from some men who were present there, the saint, whose soul had not yet departed, opened his eyes, and looked around on either side, with wonderful joy and gladness of countenance; for he was gazing upon the holy angels that had come to meet him."[27]

St Columba himself of course knew the life of both monk and hermit. In the twentieth century the image of Thomas Merton living the life of a hermit in his hermitage in the woods near the Trappist abbey of Gethsemani in Kentucky has touched many people. Numbers of men and women, lay people in the world no less than members of religious orders, are increasingly recognizing the urgent need to find a place and time to withdraw; that unless we learn to live with ourselves we cannot live with others; that solitude helps towards the fullness of our own humanity. Merton only brought to the common notice something which has always been important in the Christian tradition (and it is tempting to wonder if his fascination with Celtic monasticism did not in fact help to clarify his own search for the eremitical element within his own life). Certainly Celtic spirituality has always been clear about the role and importance of the solitary life, whether for a certain time each year, or whether for a certain period during a lifetime – for the underlying principle is that a life of activity in the world is only made possible if it is nourished by times of withdrawal into solitude and silence.

But in the end solitude is not so much a place as a state of mind and heart: it is the ability to enter into the desert of the heart, the poustinia, the inner cave of the heart, however one might wish to describe it. It is an inner attentiveness to God, a continual stream of contemplation which becomes possible even in the midst of crowds, noise, and the demands of daily life.

Pilgrims and Exiles

"We stole away because we wanted for the love of God to be on pilgrimage, we cared not where." The three Irishmen who landed in Cornwall explained their presence to King Alfred of Wessex, having drifted across the sea from Ireland for seven days in a boat made of hides, with few provisions, and without oars. Then, as now, the Celtic monks and their wanderings for the love of God caused both admiration and astonishment. In looking at the development of the *peregrinatio* (which can only be translated as a wandering form of exile and pilgrimage) we encounter one of the more extraordinary aspects of Celtic monasticism, a phenomenon which carried the intensity of the dedicated life to extremes unparalleled elsewhere in Western Christendom. These three monks were amongst the great number who for over a period of five hundred years set out to wander across the face of Europe, from Iceland to Italy. They left homeland and friends, and all life's securities, in order that they might set out into the unknown, a journey for God. They called themselves pilgrims, *peregrinati*, and dedicated themselves to go on pilgrimage for Christ's sake wherever that might take them. Most came from the monasteries of Ireland though a lesser number were from Wales, Scotland and Cornwall. The Irish first crossed the sea to Scotland, then went further afield to the continent. Most of them are unknown, though a few great names stand out – St Columcille or Columba who in the sixth century founded Iona; St Aidan who went from Iona in the seventh century to Lindisfarne, and whose monks converted Northumbria to Christianity; and St Columbanus, abbot of Bangor in the sixth century, who set out for France, and then crossed the Alps into Italy, and who at Bobbio made a foundation which was to surpass all others in fame and achievement.

They undertook this *peregrinatio* not at the prompting of any abbot or superior but because of their own inner passionate conviction that this was their destiny. St Columbanus, greatest traveller of them all, called Christians "*hospites mundi*", guests of the world. He gives the classic statement of *peregrinatio* when he speaks of it as going into exile, seeking the place of one's resurrection, the pilgrimage to heaven, the true home. "Therefore let us concern ourselves with heavenly things, not human ones, and like pilgrims always sigh for our homeland, long for our homeland. It is the end of the road that travellers look for and desire, and because we are travellers and pilgrims through this world, it is the road's end, that is of our lives, that we should always be thinking about. For that road's end is our true homeland. . . . Don't let us love the road rather than the land to which it leads, lest we lose our homeland altogether. For we have such a homeland that we ought to love it. So then, while we are on the road, as travellers, as pilgrims, as guests of the world, let us not get entangled with any earthly desires and lusts but fill our minds with heavenly and spiritual things: our theme song 'When shall I come and appear before the face of my God?'.[1] Christians must travel in perpetual pilgrimage as guests of the world."

He, and he was speaking for many other *peregrini*, looked for no sanctuary on earth, for he was seeking a heavenly country, for the love of God. As he set out from Bangor he remembered the words of God to Abraham telling him to leave his own country.[2] When the Celtic monk responded to this same call it meant that he became an exile, stripping himself of family and possessions, rooting out from heart and mind all his own aims and desires, and above all, since the Celtic love of country ran deep, the most painful of all, becoming a stranger to his homeland with no prospect of ever returning to the place of his birth.[3] It meant, in the words of a contemporary sermon, "to leave their country and their land, their riches and their worldly joys for the sake of the Lord of Creation, and go in perfect pilgrimage in imitation of Him".

To describe them as the wandering saints, though this is commonly done, is however rather misleading. They were for example entirely unlike the wandering scholars of the twelfth century, whose rootless journeying took them endlessly from place to place in search of new masters, new ideas and intellectual stimulus. But neither were they like those medieval pilgrims who after visiting a holy place or a famous shrine, would eventually return back home. This was neither aimless wandering for the sake of wandering nor was it travel to some fixed and certain destination. As Thomas Merton (a man incidentally very conscious of his own Celtic roots and fascinated by Celtic monasticism) wrote, this was not "the restless search of an unsatisfied romantic heart; it was a profound and existential tribute to realities perceived in the very structure of the world, of men and of their being."[4] The wanderlust of these Celtic monks must be seen in the context of an inner stability and an interior ascetic discipline. This is the inner journey known to all Christians but in particular to those in the monastic life, and not least to those choosing the vocation of the hermit. In the words of a ninth-century poem

All solitary in my little cell,
With not a single soul as company:
That would be pilgrimage dear to me
Before going to the meeting with death.[5]

It was said of the Welsh saint St Brynach, who had his church at Nevern in Pembrokeshire, that "by thinking nothing of the place of his birth, by forsaking his own land, he sought to find it: by living in exile he hoped to reach home."[6] What the true pilgrim sought was not any territorial possession, it was a spiritual inheritance. Here is the paradox which lies at the heart of *peregrinatio*.

To go to Rome
Is much of trouble, little of profit;
The King whom thou seekest here,
Unless thou bring Him with thee, thou wilt not find.[7]

A journey, a quest, the search for the holy, answers a deep need in all of us, the outer journey which reflects the inner journey. The twentieth century has brought easier travel and made it possible for people in their thousands to visit all the great shrines and places of pilgrimage. Even if they cannot always precisely articulate what it is that they are seeking they still find themselves drawn to holy places. The Celtic tradition of *peregrinatio* may have little in common with today's travel, yet they still have an important contribution to make towards the understanding of the purpose that underlies the journey: to find the place of one's resurrection, and the equally profound insight, that unless we also carry within our hearts the God whom we are seeking we will not find him.

There were three grades of pilgrimage or exile. The first, when a man left his country in body only, might still leave the spirit uncleansed since "it is not by path of feet not by motion of body that one draws near to God, but by practising virtues and good deeds". If travelling is purely physical then it can serve no spiritual purpose. The second was when a man was detained in his own country under authority and forced to spend his life there until death even though in zeal of heart and spirit he has left. "Since it is not for the sake of the body that they continue in their fatherland their goodwill in remaining at home avails them with the Lord as a pilgrimage." Being under restraint, under authority to an institution leaves a man free only to travel in spirit. The third was when a man left his country altogether in body and soul as the apostles did. These are the people of perfect pilgrimage, the men who can claim that they "have made pilgrimage and exile in the world, just as the elders who went before".[8] We have a chance to see what was entailed in this perfect pilgrimage, this total dedication of exile without the possibility of return, when St Brendan describes how he and his followers going round a small island saw a church built of stone and "a penitent white-faced old man praying therein, bloodless, fleshless, only a thin, wretched leather on those hard-bare bones". The old man then tells them how he came to be there. "Of the men of Ireland am I, and we were twelve men when we went on our pilgrimage; and we brought yon monstrous sea-cat with us, as a little bird, and he was very dear to us, and after that he waxed greatly, and never did any hurt to us. And eleven men of them are dead, and I am here alone, entreating thee to administer unto me Christ's Body and His Blood, and that I may then go to heaven." So, the Life continues, they gave him the sacrament and after receiving it he died and was buried there with his brethren, and in this way "the old man revealed to them the land which they were seeking, even the Land of Promise".[9]

However intense the desire and however total the commitment to undertake this exile for the love of Christ, it remained extremely costly. They all retained this intense love and longing for their native homeland whenever they were away from it. "It is the parting of the soul and the body for a man to leave his kindred and his country and go from them to strange, distant lands, in exile and perpetual pilgrimage." A small phrase in St Columba's life captures the pain of this separation. His sorrow on parting from the people he loved was hardly greater than his sorrow at leaving the seagulls and birds of Loch Fyle. "The great cry of the people of Doire has broken my heart in four." Here he is speaking for all exiles, and there have been many in the Celtic countries, not only exiles for the love of God but exiles because of hunger, land clearance, or the lack of work which has driven many thousands from their homes. Sitting on the headland of Iona which faces out across the sea to his beloved Ireland, St Columba would gaze across the ocean to the land that he had left.

Delightful to be on the hill of Howth
Before going over the white-haired sea:
The dashing of the wave against its face,
The bareness of its shores and of its border.

Delightful to be on the hill of Howth
After coming over the white-bosomed sea;
To be rowing one's little coracle,
Alas! on the wild-waved sea.

Great is the speed of my coracle,
And its stern turned upon Derry:
Grievous is my errand over the main,
Travelling to Alba of the beetling brows.

My foot in my tuneful coracle,
My sad heart tearful:
A man without guidance is weak,
Blind are all the ignorant.

There is a grey eye
That will look back upon Ireland:
It shall never see again
The men of Ireland nor her women.[10]

Perhaps this twelfth-century poem, which imagines the saint's words as
he says farewell to his Irish monastic home, catches even more
poignantly the sense of St Columba's deep sadness.

Great is the speed of my coracle,
And its stern turned upon Derry:
Grievous is my errand over the main,
Travelling to Alba of the beetling brows.

Were all Alba mine
From its centre to its border,
I would rather have the site of a house
In the middle of fair Derry.
It is for this I love Derry,
For its smoothness, for its purity;
All full of angels
Is every leaf on the oaks of Derry.

My Derry, my little oak-grove,
My dwelling and my little cell,
O living God that art in Heaven above,
Woe to him who violates it![11]

This eleventh-century poem describes a heart torn with pain and
longing.

This were pleasant, O Son of God,
with wondrous coursing
To sail back across the swelling torrent
back to Ireland.

I ever long for the land of Ireland
where I had power,
An exile now in midst of strangers,
sad and tearful.

Woe that journey forced upon me,
O King of Secrets;
Would to God I'd never gone there,
to Cooldrevne.

Well it is for the son of Dimma
in his cloister,
And happy I but were I hearing
with him in Durrow

The wind that ever plays us music
in the elm-trees
And the sudden cry of the startled blackbird,
wing a-beating.

And listen early in Ros Grencha
to stags a-belling,
And when cuckoo, at brink of summer,
joins in chorus.

I have loved the land of Ireland –
I cry for parting;
To sleep at Comgall's, visit Canice,
this were pleasant.[12]

One monk, as he bids farewell to a fellow-monk returning to Ireland,
admitted the depth of his longing to return and die in his own country.

If Christ would give me back the past,
And that first strength of days,
And that this white head of mine were dark again,
I too might go your ways.[13]

Although this had never been their original aim the *peregrini* soon began to find themselves missionaries preaching the Gospel. The interconnection of exile and mission lay of course deep in Celtic tradition, for the Word had come to Ireland through a man who himself knew the unassuageable pain of exile. St Patrick had been taken into slavery, lost his family and his home, had experienced fear and isolation, and yet out of this had learnt that exile opened up a wider world and this was where he was meant to serve Christ. So also his followers two centuries later found themselves becoming apostles for Christ and preachers of the Gospel as they encountered on their travels men and women ready to hear the Christian message. In a remarkably short time after they themselves had received the faith the Celtic world was bringing that faith back to Europe. All over the continent Christianity, which had been battered and beaten by successive waves of barbarian hordes, was given new life by men bringing the light of Christ from the west, from the furthest outpost of the Western world. "Only once in history has there been a quiet, all but imperceptible flooding of Europe by the Word of God, preached by ascetics at once rude and inspired" writes William Marnell in the opening of his study of the Irish mission, which he appropriately titled *Light from the West*.[14]

Wherever they travelled, sailing into northern seas or going on foot through Gaul and over the Alps into Italy, their poverty and total dedication made them exceedingly powerful. Their lack of monastic legislation and organization became one of their greatest assets. They had renounced power and security and so they were free, free to go anywhere and live anywhere. They needed no buildings. They were ready to feed on "nothing but herbs of the earth and water and to sleep in caves" in the words of an eighth-century Irish litany of saints.[15] As they wandered, whether alone or as part of a small group of followers, they would set up a wooden preaching cross and perhaps build one or two small cells. If the site seemed propitious they might replace wattle and daub by timber, and then perhaps by stone. A church would carry the name of its original founder, and there are still over two hundred and fifty places in Europe which commemorate the names of Celtic saints, the monks who first came there.[16] The founder might then well move on, establish further settlements as he went, until in the end he retired to some "remote place" where he would remain, engaged in prayer and contemplation until his death.[17]

The life of St Columbanus, perhaps the greatest of all the *peregrini*, is known to us because of the work of his biographer Jonas.[18] He was born between 540 and 543 and was in his late forties when he applied to his abbot for permission to go on pilgrimage. When it was granted he set out around the year 590 with a band of twelve, and journeyed through "Britannia" (scholars dispute whether this was Britain or Brittany) and on into the heart of Frankish Gaul. After the foundation of a small community in the foothills of the Vosges his fame spread and people began to seek him out, though he himself, whenever possible, stole away in search of solitude, spending time in a cave and living on wild apples and herbs. When two further centres developed he drew down upon himself the wrath of the local bishops whose approval he had failed to seek. In Ireland bishops were often functionaries of a monastery and under obedience to its abbot so he was doing nothing more than continuing a system by which monasteries and abbots did not see themselves as answerable to a bishop, but since this was never the case in Europe it was hardly surprising that episcopal authority should feel threatened. He also fell foul of them by defending the Irish dating of Easter. Summoned to appear before a synod of bishops in 603 he replied in a letter that he asked only to be allowed to live as a stranger "humble and poor for Christ's sake" amongst them. "Let Gaul I beg contain us side by side, whom the kingdom of heaven shall contain."[19] He went on to say that it was only for the sake of Christ that he had entered these lands, that he was there as a pilgrim, and that he was a *peregrinus* for life, he could never abandon this "pilgrimage for Christ". And so he continued on his way, crossing the Alps in 612 and finally, when he was in his seventies, taking part in the building of his great monastery at Bobbio. It was here, on 23rd November 612 that he died, after a life of poverty and wandering, a learned man, the author of a strongly ascetic

rule, and a poet. This is his boating song, traditionally said to have
been written as he was going up the Rhine.

> The galley, forest born, cleaves the stream,
> The dark, unbroken waves of the two-horned Rhine.
> Shout heia, lads, till the echo rings again!
> Wind driven squalls lash on us, dark as night,
> But skill and courage yet can overcome.
> Shout heia, lads, till echo rings again!
> Hold fast, for cloud and tempest pass at last,
> And brave endeavour claims the victory.[20]

While St Columbanus and many like him wandered south through
Europe other *peregrini* were facing the hazards of sea voyages through
the northern seas. Living on an island the Irish had always had a love of
the sea and their literature from earliest times told tales of voyages, and
exploration on the high seas. As they recounted the stories of the
travels of the saints the chroniclers were often making a Christianized
version of the Old Irish *imram*, a tale of mythological travel. These sea
journeys can therefore be seen as history or as allegory, and read at two
levels, either as factual accounts or as allegorical. A journey into the
unknown can become the spiritual journey which we all undertake, a
journey in which the frailty of the craft and the hazards of the ocean
become particularly apt and appropriate symbols. Of all such tales that
of Brendan remains the most extraordinary.[21]

"On this very windy and too-perilous day who can cross in safety even
this narrow strait?" On Iona the brothers asked themselves this
question as they awaited a visitor from Ireland. Even this comparatively
short crossing was frequently hazardous, with the danger of "crashing
storm and unendurably high waves".[22] We are given a very tender
picture of how these dangers were met and turned to good account
when St Columba tells his monks not to fear for St Colman as he puts
out to sea. "St Columba, while he was living in his mother church,
suddenly exclaimed with a smile: 'Colman, Beogna's son, has begun to
sail over to us, and is now in great danger in the surging tides of the
whirlpool of Brecan; and sitting in the prow he raises both hands to
heaven, and blesses the troubled and very terrible sea. But the Lord

terrifies him thus, not in order that the ship in which he sits may be overwhelmed by the waves in shipwreck, but rather to rouse him to more fervent prayer that with God's favour he may reach us after passing through the danger'."[23] Perhaps it was such an attitude of mind which made possible ventures to far greater distances and with far greater hazards. Again in the Life of St Columba we read of how Cormac was under full sail before a southerly wind for fourteen summer nights and days, holding a straight course towards the north until he seemed to pass beyond the limits of human journeying and beyond the hope of return. St Columba, though distant in body, was nevertheless present in spirit with Cormac in the ship, and at their time of greatest danger summoned the brothers into the oratory and commanded them, "Brothers, pray with your whole might for Cormac, who now in his voyage has far exceeded the bounds of human travel. Now he endures the terrors of certain horrible and monstrous things never seen before, and almost indescribable. . . ."[24]

The Faroes seem to have been discovered by Irish saints around the year 700 and inhabited by them until the second decade of the ninth century, and there is little doubt that by the eighth century they had reached Iceland. In the year 825 the monk Dicuil described an island lying to the north of Britain and said, "there are many other islands in the ocean to the north of Britain . . . on these islands hermits who have sailed from our Scotia (Ireland) have lived for roughly a hundred years".[25]

From the eighth century the Vikings presented a new peril, and prayers for protection now included the phrase "from the fury of the Northmen Good Lord deliver us".[26] But quite apart from this times were changing. The heroic, free, intensely individualistic Celtic monasticism was being challenged as the Rule of St Benedict, with its ideals of stability, balance, moderation, and above all community life, began to gain pre-eminence throughout Europe. The definite bias that grew up against the whole idea of *peregrinatio* is nicely caught in this twelfth-century Irish tale from the *Lives of Mochuda*. It tells how Mochuda resolved that he would no longer remain in his monastery but "leave Ireland, and I will not be two nights in one place, but I will be in penance throughout the length of the great world". The following day he sought out Comgall and after blessing one another Comgall told him to sit down. The *Life* continues, " 'I would rather not,' said Mochuda, 'for I am in a hurry; there is a ship about to sail,' said he, 'and I must go in her.' 'Not so', said Comgall, 'for God will cause the ship to remain here tonight.' So Mochuda sat down, and his shoes were taken off him and as they were taken off Comgall said: 'Come out, O devil,' he said, 'from the shoe; thou shalt not carry off any more spoil which thou didst find.' The devil thereupon departed, and Comgall said to the saint that he should return home, and attend to his hours. And he said:

It is good for a clerk to reside in one place
And attend the (canonical) hours.
It is mocking devils that put
The spirit of restlessness in a man.

So Mochuda continued to reside without wandering through the power of God and Comgall."[27]

the

---

celebration
of
creation

The Universe

St Patrick had himself learnt to pray out of doors in those first ten years of his life when he was in Ireland as a slave looking after the herds in all sorts of weather. He tells us enough of this in The Confession for us to see how he wrestled with the elements and made this into prayer. "I used to remain even in the woods and in the mountains: before daylight I used to rise to prayer, through snow, through frost, through rain, and felt no harm." In a day he would say about a hundred prayers, and in the night the same. This is the kind of praying that unites a man with the earth.[1] According to tradition he was questioned about his faith by two heathen princesses, daughters of the high king of Laoghaire. "Who is God? Of whom is God?" they asked. "Where is his dwelling? . . . How will he be seen, how is he loved, how is he found?" The dialogue which ensued took the form of a great creation-oriented credo, very different in its emphasis to the redemption focus found in the Nicene and other western creeds.

Our God, God of all men,
God of heaven and earth, seas and rivers,
God of sun and moon, of all the stars,
God of high mountain and lowly valleys,
God over heaven, and in heaven, and under heaven.
He has a dwelling in heaven and earth and sea
and in all things that are in them.

He inspires all things, he quickens all things.
He is over all things, he supports all things.

He makes the light of the sun to shine,
He surrounds the moon and the stars,

He has made wells in the arid earth,
Placed dry islands in the sea.
He has a Son co-eternal with himself . . .
And the Holy Spirit breathes in them;
Not separate are the Father and the Son and Holy Spirit.[2]

Here we see St Patrick speaking in terms that would have resonance with his heathen hearers: the pre-Christian love of creation as good. The perception of the holiness of the earth and the sacredness of matter belonged to the world familiar to them, the world in which the natural and the divine still met. Elsewhere in Europe the Christian Church was fulminating against the natural world, imposing its strictures on the landscape, cutting down sacred trees, despoiling sacred wells, and denying the natural rhythm that depended on the slow turning of the sun and moon and planets. The anti-pagan polemic and admonitions of the councils in sixth-century Gaul and Spain, which were nothing less than a conflict in the relationship between man and nature, had no place in the Celtic approach to God.[3]

Blathmac, of whom virtually nothing is known except that he was a monk writing in the years around 750-70, composed a great epic poem in which he re-told the whole story of creation and redemption. He saw every creature, men and women, animals and angels, the world in its totality, in relation to the creator, "lord without beginning and lord without any end". This is the God who is the king of the heavens, his is the brightly clothed sun, and his the gleaming moon. He marks out the seven heavens, and strews the skies with beautiful stars. He can raise a mighty wind that tears a forest from its stout roots; he can raise the waves so that they drown the tops of proud ships.

His is the earth to his will; it is he who moves the sea: both has he endowed, the one with plants and the other with sea-creatures.

He is the most generous that exists; he is a hospitaller in possessions; his is every flock that he sees, his the wild beasts and the tame.

Then come stanzas that are addressed to Mary.

Your son of fair fame owns every bird that spreads wings; on wood, on land, on clear pool, it is he who gives them joy.

Your son Christ, it is clear, is one of the three persons of the deity, and all things, indeed, have been created by him.

To your son is sung our constant hymn, his praises at every hour: "Holy, holy, holy, pure is the Lord, God of hosts."[4]

"Thus is sung the eternal hymn that has never withered away . . ." He will write as vividly and as movingly of the crucifixion.[5] The idea that the world was brought into being in order that through its study the character of the creator might be learnt, is a very powerful concept in much of this early Irish writing. Creation reveals God. It is as though the world is the teacher who sets forth and preaches God, "the elements sound and show forth the knowledge of God through the work that they do".[6]

One of the most important religious poems of early Ireland, the Saltair na Rann, or psalter of the verses, is so called because it is divided, like the psalter, into one hundred and fifty verses. It is ascribed to Oengus the Culdee (or hermit) in the early ninth century although its language suggests it may belong to the tenth. It opens with a magnificent piece of writing, an account of creation which sees God as the king who is actively, physically engaged in the making of his world, forming and fashioning, shaping and hewing it. The concrete, specific titles given to God, and the choice of verbs used, are significant. They reflect a sense that all things in creation owe their architecture, shape, design to a God who is carpenter, maker, artist, designer, one who creates by moulding, shaping, fashioning.

My own King, King of the pure heavens,
Without pride, without contention
who didst create the folded world,
my King ever-living, ever victorious.

King above the elements, surpassing the sun,
King above the ocean depths,
King in the south and the north, in the west and east,
with whom no contention can be made.

King of the Mysteries, who wast and art,
before the elements, before the ages,
King yet eternal, comely his aspect,
King without beginning, without end.

King who created lustrous heaven,
who is not arrogant, not overweaning,
and the earth with its multitudinous delights,
strong, powerful, stable.

King who didst make the noble brightness,
and the darkness, with its gloom;
the one, the perfect day,
the other, the perfect night.

King who fashioned the vast deeps
out of the primary stuff of the elements,
who . . .
the formless mass.

King who formed out of it each element,
who confirmed them without restriction, a lovely mystery,
both tempestuous and serene,
both animate and inanimate.

King who hewed gloriously, with energy,
out of the very shapely primal stuff,
the heavy, round earth
with foundations, length and breadth.

King who shaped within no narrow limits
in the circle of the firmament
the globe, fashioned
like a goodly apple, truly round.

King who formed after that with fixity
the fresh masses about the earth;
the very smooth currents above the world
of the chill, watery air.

King who didst sift the cold excellent water
on the earth-mass of the noble cliffs
into rills, with the reservoirs of the streams,
according to their measure, with moderation.[7]

No-one lived closer to nature than the monks, and in particular of
course the hermits. St Ciaran of Clonmacnois died looking up at the
wide skies, lying on the green turf of his monastery beside the river.
Their lives became intertwined with the times and colours and rhythms
of the world around them. They read the psalms and said the hours in
peace with the birds. They lived close to the sound of the wind in the
trees, the changing light of night and day, the cries of the birds. They
ate berries, nuts and herbs and drank water from the spring. It was a life
of renunciation and yet a life that was totally fulfilled. Marvan, brother
of king Gooary of Connaught, who died around the year 663, had
renounced the life of a warrior-prince for that of a hermit, but when the
king tried to persuade him to return to the court he was quite clear
about his chosen way of life. The poem takes the form of a colloquy
between the brothers.

Gooary:
Why, hermit Marvan, sleepest thou not
Upon a feather quilt?
Why sleepest thou abroad
Upon a pitchpine floor?

Marvan:
I have a hut in the wood:
Only my Lord knows it;
An ash tree closes it on one side,
And a hazel like a great tree by a rath on the other.

The size of my hut, small, not too small,
A homestead with familiar paths.
From its gable a she-bird sings
A sweet song in her thrush's cloak.

A tree of apples of great bounty,
Like a mansion, stout:
A pretty bush, thick as a fist,
Of small hazel-nuts,
Branching and green.

Fair white birds come, herons, seagulls,
The sea sings to them,
No mournful music:
Brown grouse from the russet heather.

The sound of the wind against a branching wood,
Grey cloud, riverfalls,
The cry of the swan,
Delightful music![8]

"Though you relish that which you enjoy exceeding all wealth I am content with that which is given me by my gentle Christ." This is the whole philosophy of the hermit life. These are men who see what lies around them, see that it is good: the ground to be cared for, fruits collected, fish netted, all the practical things making for a fulfilling relationship with the earth and preventing escape into a wilderness of their own fantasies. Here is real contentment. The hermit who says his prayers and reads his psalms in peace among the birds is clear that he would not exchange his small oratory for any other household. A ninth-century lyric tells how the writer has found all the shelter that his heart could desire.

> A full household could not be more lovely than my little oratory in Tuaim Inbir with its stars in their order, with its sun and its moon.

> That you may be told its story, it was a craftsman who made it – my little heart-God from heaven, he is the thatcher who thatched it.

> A house where rain does not pour, a place where spear-points are not dreaded, as bright as in a garden with no fence about it.[9]

God the Creator has here become the craftsman who has roofed the house, and set in it the sun and the moon as two great lamps. These poems which were written by the early Irish hermits continually startle us by the strong feelings that they reveal, and the extraordinary emotional insights they bring. They do not write descriptive verse, the conventional nature poetry of a later age. There is nothing romantic or mystical in this writing. As we read it it often produces a shock of delight in us because of this imaginative treatment which sets it apart from so much classical or medieval nature poetry. "Pleasant is the glittering of the sun today upon these margins because it flickers so." An Irish scribe scribbled the lines in an idle moment in the margin of the volume of Cassiodorus that he was copying. It is the emotion that matters – that sudden impulse to record what he saw and felt.

These early Celtic scribes and hermits lived, by the destiny of their dedication to a life of prayer and solitude, in places of great beauty, and they brought to their environment eyes washed miraculously clear by continual contemplation. As Robin Flower has said "they first in Europe had that strange vision of natural things in an almost unnatural purity". There is a clarity and an economy in their style, a quality of rapidity and joyousness. It has the secret of keeping the reader's mind alert and happy – possibly something they learnt from the story-tellers of an earlier age. The skill lies in never saying more than is necessary, in streamlining, in leaving much unsaid or half said. They pass rapidly over the abstract and discursive phrases and instead concentrate on the concrete image or fact. This brings to their writing an almost haiku-like quality, something which recalls the artistry of the impressionist painter who knows how to handle his short brush strokes so effectively. The result is poetry which is "all fire and air, praise and prayer and dedication of the heart".[10]

O Son of the living God, old eternal King, I desire a hidden hut in the wilderness that it may be my home.

A narrow little blue stream beside it and a clear pool for the washing away of sin through the grace of the Holy Ghost,

A lovely wood close about it on every side, to nurse the birds with all sorts of voices and to hide them with its shelter,

Looking south for heat, and a stream through its land, and good fertile soil suitable for all plants,

A beautiful draped church, a home for God from Heaven, and bright lights above the clean white Gospels,

Enough of clothing and food from the king of fair fame, and to be sitting for a while and praying to God in every place.[11]

This is nature poetry transfigured; all things seen through contemplative prayer and through love. The scribe in the wood in this eighth- or ninth-century poem writes out of his sense of gratitude for what has been given to him.

The woodland thicket overtops me,
the blackbird sings me a lay, praise I will not conceal:
above my lined little booklet
the trilling of birds sings to me.

The clear cuckoo sings to me, lovely discourse,
in its grey cloak from the crest of the bushes;
truly – may the Lord protect me! –
well do I write under the forest wood.[12]

In our own day Thomas Merton writing about the hermit life from his own experience in the woods near the Cistercian abbey of Gethsemani in Kentucky has brought to many people an awareness of what that life is.[13] John Howard Griffin, who went to live in Merton's hermitage after his death, kept a journal of his time there. "The very nature of your solitude involves you in union with the prayers of the wind in the trees, the movement of the stars, the feeding of the birds in the fields, the building of the anthills. You witness the creator and attend to him in all his creation." And then he goes on to find, what generations of earlier Celtic solitaries knew, "This is not for one moment mere pantheism. You do not 'worship' the thing, but the creator of the thing. The thing fascinates precisely because it raises your attention through its beauty or interest above itself to the creator. . . ."[14] He was discovering, just as the earlier hermits had, that he was being brought back all the time to a deeper sense of unity with God, and with the whole of his world.

A theological basis for this spirituality which emphasized the immanence of God was provided by John Scotus Eriguena (810-877) the greatest thinker that the Celtic Church produced. His major work, *De Naturae Divisione* says that God is in all things and is said to be the true essence of all things. One of his favourite words is theophany, and for him the world is a theophany. Things are not external to God, for with him "making" is the same as "being".[15]

The Celtic experience was thus of a religious universe. It is not static or dead, but a dynamic, living, powerful universe, reflecting a power which comes ultimately from God. Men and women establish a relationship with this universe, speaking to it, listening, trying to create a harmony – for they are at its centre. God has created things in an orderly fashion, and imposed on the world an order which holds it together, in which men and women have their place and role. Credal hymns and litanies celebrate the totality of creation and affirm a personal involvement with it, so that God and his universe, plants and animals, men and women, all bound together in the unity of one created order, were a very important part of this heritage. They were carried down by word of mouth in oral tradition, handed on from one generation to another. When Alexander Carmichael travelled throughout the highlands and the western isles of Scotland at the end of the last century collecting this material he was struck as he went into the house of these simple crofting and fishing people to hear how they spoke of the great God of life, the father of all living. They addressed him "with all the awe and deference due to the great Chief whom they wish to approach and attract" and yet also in language which was simple, homely and dignified. One woman told him how every child learnt from its mother at an early age to take part in this act of praise. "My mother would be asking us to sing our morning song to God down in the back-house, as Mary's lark was singing it up in the clouds and as Christ's mavis was singing it yonder in the tree, giving glory to God of the creatures for the repose of the night, for the light of the day, and for the joy of life. She would tell us that every creature on the earth here below and in the ocean beneath and in the air above was giving glory to the great God of the creatures and the worlds, of the virtues and the blessings, and would we be dumb!"[16]

I believe, O God of all gods,
That Thou art the eternal Father of life;
I believe, O God of all gods,
That Thou art the eternal Father of love.

These are the opening lines of a great credal hymn which begins by celebrating the totality of creation, first the universe itself, and then comes to each individual element, and each individual person within that universe. The image that is used for the making of the person is a homely and familiar one, taken from the weaving of cloth.

I believe, O Lord and God of the peoples,
That Thou art the creator of the high heavens,
That thou art the creator of the skies above,
That Thou art the creator of the oceans below.

I believe, O Lord and God of the peoples,
That Thou art He Who created my soul and set its warp.

Who created my body from dust and from ashes,
Who gave to my body breath, and to my soul its possession.

This then moves into a hymn of praise which becomes an act of worship.

> I am giving Thee worship with my whole life,
> I am giving Thee assent with my whole power,
> I am giving Thee praise with my whole tongue,
> I am giving Thee honour with my whole utterance.
> I am giving Thee reverence with my whole understanding,
> I am giving Thee offering with my whole thought,
> I am giving Thee praise with my whole fervour,
> I am giving Thee humility in the blood of the Lamb.
>
> I am giving Thee love with my whole devotion,
> I am giving Thee kneeling with my whole desire,
> I am giving Thee love with my whole heart,
> I am giving Thee affection with my whole sense;
> I am giving Thee my existence with my whole mind,
> I am giving Thee my soul, O God of all gods.[17]

The sense of wonder which is both awe at the power of the creator God and delight in his ingenuity and generosity, brings a response of gratitude. Blathmac had said, "He is the most generous that exists", and had then gone on, in a vivid phrase, to speak of him as a "hospitaller in possessions", an image that would mean a great deal in a society which held hospitality to be one of the great virtues. One of the morning prayers from the Outer Hebrides opens

> Each day may I remember the source of the mercies
> Thou hast bestowed on me gently and generously;
>
> Each thing I have received from Thee it came,
> Each thing for which I hope, from Thy love it will come,
> Each thing I enjoy, it is of Thy bounty,
> Each thing I ask, comes of Thy disposing.[18]

78

Another prayer says

> Thanks be to Thee, Jesu Christ,
> For the many gifts Thou hast bestowed on me,
> Each day and night, each sea and land,
> Each weather fair, each calm, each wild. [19]

Gratefulness of this sort prevents possessiveness, the desire to own, to retain. Instead there is detachment, the readiness to give up the attempt to possess and exploit, to hold onto things, to use them for our own purposes. Whereas Tennyson will pluck the flower from the wall, root and all, and hold it in his hand, hoping thereby to know something of the mystery of God, the Celtic approach will never be to wrench anything from the ground, the place where it belongs. Hermit poetry comes from men living lives of renunciation, and still today it challenges the values of materialism and consumerism, for it grows out of a world in which everything is respected for its own sake, and given the space and freedom to be itself.

For there is never any confusion between the Creator and the world of his creating. God is involved in his creation, and is close to everything that he has made in his world, but there is here a vision of creation which yet avoids pantheism. In this, once again, we find distinct echoes of the East. Gregory of Nyssa or Basil the Great see creation as a revelation of the presence of God, but they are careful to preserve the distinction of the two and insist on their separateness. This remains the emphasis in the Celtic approach to the world. It is given expression in this hymn in which a woman on the isle of Harris gives thanks to God after she has cured herself of leprosy by using aright the healing plants and fishes of the island. She recognizes that there is a right balance to be maintained between herself and the physical world. Everything good comes from God and is to be given freedom to be itself, to enjoy and to be enjoyed. We are enslaved if we care for anything in ways that exclude the giver. So there is a sense of common creation, by which men and women, plants and animals, the Trinity and the heavenly powers, are all bound together, and the only response to this can be one of praise.

It were as easy for Jesu
To renew the withered tree
As to wither the new
Were it His will to do so.
    Jesu! Jesu! Jesu!
    Jesu! meet it were to praise Him.

There is no plant in the ground
But it is full of His virtue,
There is no form in the strand
But it is full of His blessing.
    Jesu! Jesu! Jesu!
    Jesu! meet it were to praise Him.

There is no life in the sea,
There is no creature in the river,
There is naught in the firmament
But proclaims His goodness.
    Jesu! Jesu! Jesu!
    Jesu! meet it were to praise Him.

There is no bird on the wing,
There is no star in the sky,
There is nothing beneath the sun
But proclaims His goodness.
    Jesu! Jesu! Jesu!
    Jesu! meet it were to praise Him.[20]

One of the most striking qualities of the Christian poetry of Wales in recent years has been the way in which it has succeeded in conveying again this same vision, the sense of excitement of what God the craftsman has wrought on his earth. Gwenallt tells us

God has not forbidden us to love the world
And to love man and all his works,
To love it with all the naked senses together,
Every shape and colour, every voice and every sound.
There is a shudder in our blood when we see
The traces of his craftsman's hands upon the world . . .[21]

Because the writer sees all things in their own specific natures he also sees the creative power and wisdom of God flowing through them. Today, as pollution and exploitation and greed devalue and damage the earth it becomes more and more difficult to find the presence of God mediated in and through his world. But with the increasing sense of urgency of the need to regain some respect for the earth while there is still time, it may be that the Celtic vision of creation will be re-discovered. Perhaps if it had not been lost things would not be as serious as they are. The matter with the world is matter, as George MacLeod says.

Over half a century ago H. J. Massingham, the English writer on rural affairs, was saying that if only the Celtic Church had survived it is possible that the "fissure between Christianity and nature, widening through the centuries, would not have cracked the unity of western man's attitude to the universe."[22] Creation spirituality, which the Church is discovering at the same time as the world of politics is discovering ecology and a green platform, has been there in fact all the time in the Celtic tradition, and we have paid the price for the neglect of that heritage. When we cut ourselves off from the earth we are impoverished, whether as individuals or as society as a whole. Again the Celtic speaks of something which is basic, is universal. It is an awareness which is found amongst indigenous peoples, known for example to African or native American peoples while it has been forgotten in the West. A world which has lost its vision of the sacredness of creation has also lost its commitment to the dignity of human life. Only now is our western society becoming aware of living on a planet of which we are a apart, and that God the creator and redeemer is at work with the whole of his creation.

Common Creation

"The Lord is indeed good to me", exclaims the hermit as he sits with his open book under a hedge of trees, and listens to the birds.

> The chanting of birds I hear –
> Good to draw man's tears:
> Each of them answers the other:
> Does not the whole Church do so?

In this poem, which is dated to about the year 806, the writer is clearly conversant with the times of the year at which the birds begin to sing, and he sees them as singing the responses and joining in the canonical hours with him.

> The birds of the world, power without ill,
> come to welcome the sun,
> On January's nones, at the different hours,
> The cry of the host from the dark wood.

> On the eighth calends of noble April
> The swallows come on their pure tryst,
> (Till they depart)
> On the eighth calends of October.

> On the festival of Ciaran, son of the carpenter,
> Wild geese come over the cold sea,
> On the festival of Cyprian, a great counsel,
> The brown stag bells from the ruddy field.

Melodious music the birds perform
to the King of the heaven of the clouds,
Praising the radiant King
Hark from afar the choir of the birds.[1]

"Understand, if you want to know the Creator, created things." When
St Columbanus said this he was speaking out of his own experience.
The integration of humankind with the birds and the animals as part of
a common creation was something the Celtic world not only grasped
intellectually and affectively but also lived out as well. Jonas, the
biographer of St Columbanus, tells how during his periods of fasting
and prayer in solitary places, the saint would call the beasts and the
birds to him as he walked, and how they would come straightaway,
rejoicing and gambolling around him in great delight would behave
"like little puppies around their master". He would summon a squirrel
from the tree tops and let it climb all over him, and from time to time its
head might be seen peeping through the folds of his robes. On one
occasion when twelve wolves came up to him he stood still, motionless
and fearless, repeating a verse of the psalm "O God be not far from me"
until, after sniffing at his garments, they went peacefully away. Even
the bears respected him, and so gentle was he that his gentleness
communicated itself to them and they obeyed him. One bear was
persuaded by him to leave its cave so that he could make it his
hermitage; another, which was preparing to eat a dead stag, left it so
that St Columbanus could have the hide as leather for his monks. On
another occasion the brothers, getting ready to pick the plums, found a
bear already there and it seemed as though nothing would be left for
them, but St Columbanus decided that they must be shared, one part
for the bear and the other for the monks.[2]

Bears and wolves, animals that in most cultures would be hunted
down without pity, are here shown warmth and gentleness by these
men of prayer, and the animals respond in kind. In the Celtic tradition
there are many legends which tell of the warm and fulfilling relationships established between monks who chose a life of solitude, and the
wild animals of the forests amongst whom they lived. In fact it was
often the animals themselves who led the hermits to the places in
which they eventually settled. It might start with a dream, followed by

the encounter itself. St Brynach was told by an angel in a vision to go along the river bank until he saw "a wild white sow with white piglings" and they would show him the spot for his hermitage.[3] To follow a stag, a boar or a pig was in fact of course a shrewd move on the part of any intending hermit since the animals would eventually make for a water supply. Here, behind the legend, lies the element of sensible reality, the familiarity that men living close to nature acquire for the ways of the natural world. Sometimes an animal which had helped a monk in the building of his cell would then stay on, become his helpmate and share his life with him. When St Ciaran began to dig the cemetery at Saighir all by himself he saw a wild boar coming towards him which of its own accord set to work energetically with its tusks to clear and level the ground, and then to help with the construction of a hut. After this it stayed on to become his servant, and soon other animals came from their lairs, a fox, a badger and a deer, and "they remained with him in the greatest docility, for they obeyed the orders of the holy man in everything like monks". One day however the fox, "who was more cunning and wily than the other animals", reverted to his former ways and, tired of his vegetarian diet, succumbed to the temptation, stole his master's shoes and took them to his old den in the wilderness, intending to devour them there. The story then continues with its gentle and kindly account of his backsliding, his repentance and his restoration. "Learning this the holy father Ciaran sent another monk or pupil, namely the Badger, to the wilderness after the Fox to bring back the brother to his place. And the Badger, who was well acquainted with the woods, obeying at once the word of his superior, set out and came straight to the cave of brother Fox; and when he found him about to devour the shoes of his master, he cut off his ears and tail and plucked out his hairs and compelled him to come with him to the monastery to do penance for his theft. And the Fox, compelled perforce, came along with the Badger to St Ciaran in his cell at nones, bringing the shoes unharmed. And the holy man said to the Fox, 'Why have you done this sin, brother, which monks ought not to do? Behold, our water is pure and common to all, and the food likewise is apportioned to all in common; and if you had desired to eat flesh according to your instinct, almighty God would have made it for us from the bark of trees.' Then the Fox, begging for forgiveness, did penance by fasting, and did not touch food till the holy man commanded it. Thereupon he remained in the fellowship of the others."[4]

Mo Chua, a contemporary of St Columba, lived in a hermitage in the wilderness with no worldly wealth except for three creatures, a cock and a mouse and a fly. The cock's work was to keep matins for him at midnight. The mouse would not allow him to sleep more than five hours in a day and a night, and when he wanted to sleep longer, tired from many long prayers, the mouse would begin nibbling his ear and so awake him. The work that the fly did for him was to walk along every line he read in his psalter, and when he rested from singing his psalms stay on the line he had left until he returned. After a time when these three creatures died, Mo Chua wrote to St Columba in Iona and complained of the death of his flock. And St Columba replying said to him, "Brother, you must not wonder at the death of the flock that has gone from you, for misfortune never comes but where there are riches."[5]

The range and variety of services that legend records the birds and animals performing for the monks is almost endless. At Glendalough St Kevin comes to rely on the friendly badger to bring him a salmon daily, and it also once rescued his precious psalter unharmed when it fell into the water of the lake. A bird drops a feather to make a pen for St Molaisse of Devenish when he wants to write a book. A stag holds a book open on its antlers so that St Cainnech of Aghaboe may study while he is in the forest. St Finnian of Clonard harnesses wild deer to pull a wagon loaded with timber. Because St Ciaran of Clonmacnois dealt so gently with the fox and it often used to visit him, he persuaded it to carry his psalter between him and his tutor. "And the fox used to be humbly attending the lesson until the writing of it on wax came to an end, and then he would take it with him to Ciaran." On one occasion however "his natural malice broke through the fox, and he began to eat his book for he was greedy about the leather bands that were about it on the outside". Suddenly a band of hunters came upon him, and he could find no shelter anywhere except under St Ciaran's cowl. "So God's name was magnified, as was Ciaran's, by the saving of the book from the fox and the fox from the hounds."[6] Thus the support and help is mutual. There is a balance between the humans and the natural creatures, and both in turn show kindliness to one another. This story is told of St Kevin. "At one Lenten session, St Kevin, as was his way, fled from the company of men to a certain solitude, and in a little hut that did but keep out the sun and the rain, gave himself earnestly to reading and to prayer, and his leisure to contemplation alone. And as he knelt in his accustomed fashion, with his hand outstretched through the window and lifted up to heaven, a blackbird settled on it, and busying herself as in her nest, laid in it an egg. And so moved was the saint that in all patience and gentleness he remained, neither closing nor withdrawing his hand: but until the young ones were fully hatched he held it out unwearied, shaping it for the purpose. And for a sign of perpetual remembrance of this thing, all the images of St Kevin throughout Ireland show a blackbird in his outstretched hand."[7]

Perhaps the best known known example of the trust and sympathy that can develop between humans and animals is the friendship of a monk for his cat Pangur. In this charming ninth century poem the writer finds Pangur's "childish craft" of mousing parallels his own attempts at solving the problems of scholarship.

> I and Pangur Ban my cat,
> 'Tis a like task we are at:
> Hunting mice is his delight,
> Hunting words I sit all night.
>
> Better far than praise of men
> 'Tis to sit with book and pen;
> Pangur bears me no ill will,
> He too plies his simple skill.
>
> 'Tis a merry thing to see
> At our tasks how glad are we,
> When at home we sit and find
> Entertainment to our mind.
>
> Oftentimes a mouse will stray
> In the hero Pangur's way;
> Oftentimes my keen thought set
> Takes a meaning in its net.

'Gainst the wall he set his eye
Full and fierce and sharp and sly;
'Gainst the wall of knowledge I
All my little wisdom try.

When a mouse darts from its den
O how glad is Pangur then!
O what gladness do I prove
When I solve the doubts I love!

So in peace our tasks we ply,
Pangur Ban, my cat, and I;
In our arts we find our bliss,
I have mine and he has his.

Practice every day has made
Pangur perfect in his trade;
I get wisdom day and night
Turning darkness into light.[8]

The friendship of the animals for their human companions and
benefactors was also extended to one another. The creatures learn
through their relationships with the humans to become brothers and
sisters to one other. Under St Brynach's tutelage a wolf was designated
as the keeper of a cow, her herdsman to drive her to the pastures every
morning and in the evening to bring her safely home. When a
neighbouring king on a journey was refused supper by the saint and took
revenge by putting the cow into his pot the wolf ran to his master, and
"sad and sighing lay prostrate on the ground" until the miracle-working
saint restored the cow to life and returned it to the safekeeping of the
wolf.[9] The natural cruelty and savagery among wild birds and animals is
reversed. One day a kite seized one of the tame pigeons which used to
fly down to St Tatheus and play on his table. The saint grieved, but
hoped that it would be restored. He waited until the next day after mass
when the rapacious kite descended, holding the pigeon in its claws, and
laid it free and safe before the feet of the holy man, who exclaimed,
"See the pigeon now lives that late was dead; she flies and plays . . . I

praise the Creator, who has given me this bird, has sent it to me from the strong-winged kite."[10]

Another story about St Kevin tells how when he needed milk for a foster-child a doe with her fawn came down from the mountain daily and was milked for the child. All went well until one day a wolf killed the fawn and then of course the doe failed to give the milk. St Kevin thereupon commanded, "Let the animal who did the disservice, do service". The wolf came down the mountain and, settling himself on his paws before the doe, the doe licked him and gave her milk at the sight of him. "So the wolf could come at every milking time: and the doe would be milked in his presence."[11]

Legends such as these are endless and make delightful reading. But their charm should not be allowed to blind us to the profound truth which they reveal. In some mysterious way we see at work here mutual love, trust and sympathy which breaks down barriers and brings about a glimpse of that common redemption which is promised to the world in Romans VIII.

Of all these stories none is more delightful than that account which we find in Bede of St Cuthbert's walk along the beach on the isle of Lindisfarne at night. He is watched by a hidden observer who reported that there followed in his footsteps too little otters who prostrated themselves on the sand, licking his feet, warming them with their breath and trying to dry them with their fur. The thought of those small, furry animals, rubbing themselves round his ankles as he emerges frozen from the North Sea after long hours of prayer makes a pleasing picture and it is tempting to let it remain at that level. But Bede himself would have seen it differently. He would have placed over it the lens of the Scriptures. He uses the words of the Gospel spoken by Jesus after the transfiguration: "Tell the vision to no man". It was a moment of such awe and terror that the observer, like the disciples, was "stricken with deadly fear". He had not been watching a man on a beach with his pets; he had seen the face of Christ in a man so transfigured in prayer that the right order of creation was in him restored. For Bede St Cuthbert was the new Adam, once more at peace with all creation.[12]

Many of these saints and hermits who went into the desert places of coast or forest, the deserted places where they find God in the solitude of their hearts, must have known the ancient teachings of the Church which told them they had within themselves the sun and the moon and the stars – the whole of creation. "You yourself are even another little world." The words of a homily of Origen express a vision of the human person as a microcosm which is one of the most universal of human insights, but which is particularly strong in Eastern spirituality. "The heart is but a small vessel", wrote St Macarius, "and yet dragons and lions are there, and there poisonous creatures and all the treasures of wickedness; rough uneven places are there, and gaping chasms. There likewise is God, there are the angels, there life and the Kingdom, the light and the apostles . . . all things are there."[13] It is hardly surprising that such cosmic awareness should find echoes with the Celtic saints even though they were themselves not so much interested in abstract speculation. Yet they knew from their own experience, and from the kind of life that they lived, something of the answer to that question of Isaac the Syrian "What is a charitable heart?" for they were themselves a living answer. "A heart which burns for all creation, for human beings and birds and animals and demons, and for every creature. He who has such a heart cannot see or call to mind a creature without his eyes becoming filled with tears by reason of the immense compassion which seizes his heart . . . that is why such a man never ceases to pray also for the animals."[14] Here is a real opening up to the whole universe, to the birds and the animals no less than the sun, the moon and the stars, as well as to men and women. All become brothers and sisters, part of common creation. And also, in some mysterious way, in relating to them there is the discovery that this is also relating to the whole of oneself, that one is fraternizing with obscure parts of oneself, with one's own depths. Then the inner world becomes as large as the outer, a world without walls and without frontiers.

Healing

"Great is the virtue that is in the plants of the ground and in the fruits of the sea, were we but to hold them in esteem and turn them to good use – O King, great indeed! The Being of life never set a thing in the creation of the universe, but He set some good with it – He never did; O King, many a good is in the soil of the earth and in the depth of the sea did we but know how to make good use of them."[1] The old crofter in the Outer Hebrides who said this to Alexander Carmichael spoke for all those Celtic people who lived close to nature, and knew its gifts and its powers. They approached the natural world with a feeling of familiarity but also at the same time with a sense of reverence and awe. Carmichael described a shepherd who had spent his life in close communion with nature and who loved the plants as he loved his own children "with a warm abiding love which no poverty could cool and no age could dim".[2] At the heart of this deep love lay the recognition that all good things in the natural world come from God and reflect the goodness of their creator, and so their healing properties could never be disassociated from the power of God himself to will that healing. There is no pantheism here, for everything points beyond itself to the creator God. The woman on Harris who cured herself of leprosy by the right use of plants and fish recognized this when she expressed her gratitude in a hymn of praise.

> There is no plant in the ground
> But is full of His virtue,
> There is no form in the strand
> But is full of His blessing.[3]

Many of the plants and trees that were known to have healing properties were thought to have acquired them through association with Christ during his time on earth. There were however a small number of plants which could never be forgiven for their ungracious conduct to the Gracious One and as a result their use in healing was "crossed" or forbidden. The thorn-tree could never be forgiven because of its prickly pride in allowing itself to have been made into a crown for the King of kings; the fig-tree because of its inhospitality to Christ; the reed because it had carried the sponge dipped in vinegar. The aspen tree was particularly loathed. People would look at the quivering and quaking of its leaves even in the stillest air and be reminded of its guilty secret – that it had haughtily held up its head while all the other trees of the forest had bowed down their heads as the King of all created things was being led to Calvary, proud that it had been chosen by the enemies of Christ as the wood for the cross on which the Saviour of the world was to be crucified. Clods and stones and other missiles, as well as curses, would be hurled at it. No crofter on Uist would use aspen for his plough or any farming implement, nor would a fisherman use aspen about his boat or any of his fishing gear. The man who gave these verses to Alexander Carmichael told him that he always took off his bonnet and cursed the tree whenever he saw it.

Malison be on thee, O aspen tree!
On thee was crucified the King of the mountains,
In whom were driven the nails without clench,
And that driving crucifying was exceeding sore –
That driving crucifying was exceeding sore.

Malison be on thee, O aspen hard!
On thee was crucified the King of glory,
Sacrifice of Truth, Lamb without blemish,
His blood in streams down pouring –
His blood in streams down pouring.

Malison be on thee, O aspen cursed!
On thee was crucified the King of kings,
And malison be on the eye that seeth thee,
If it maledict thee not, thou aspen cursed –
If it maledict thee not, thou aspen cursed.[4]

In contrast, the pearlwort, that small plant found on the moors and the hills, was a cherished plant, blessed by its happy association with Christ in his earthly life. Some said that it was the first plant on which Christ placed his foot when he came to earth; others that it was the first plant on which he placed his foot after he rose from the dead, and a third tradition maintained that it was the plant on which Christ lay when he was "out and away from his enemies". It was believed that when it was placed over the lintel of a door it prevented any evil spirits from entering the house and from beguiling or carrying away any members of the household. When it was placed under the right knee of a woman in labour (providing that she first removed from her fingers any rings which might check or divert its influence) it would have a soothing effect, bringing her relief and ensuring that neither she nor her child would be spirited away by the fairies.

In the Highlands of Scotland people maintained that there were twenty-four diseases inherent in men and beasts, caused by minute microbes, "miserable, full of spite, venom and hostility". They had no idea how they inherited these diseases, though they thought that certain animals and certain families were afflicted more than others, and that this was due to their own, and their forebears', long continuance in offending God. But they also believed that Christ, "the Physician of virtues and blessings", by his words and actions could repulse the sinister microbes responsible for this suffering and bring back wholeness and health.

Because Christ himself had walked the earth, curing all manner of diseases, restoring the sick and bringing health to those who were suffering, healing becomes possible for men and women today. A woman on Mull can sing this song which celebrates the Christ who knows how to heal every sort of wound and hurt.

He Who so calmly rode
The little ass fair of form,
Who healed each hurt and bloody wound
That clave to the people of every age:

He made glad the sad and the outcast,
He gave the rest to the restless and the tired,
He made free the bond and the unruly,
Each old and young in the land.

He opened the eyes of the blind,
He awakened the step of the lame,
He loosed the tongue that was dumb,
He gave life to him that was dead.

He stemmed the fierce-rushing blood,
He took the keen prickle from the eye,
He drank the draught that was bitter,
Trusting to the High Father of heaven.

He gave strength to Peter and Paul,
He gave strength to the Mother of tears,
He gave strength to Brigit of the flocks,
Each joint and bone and sinew.[5]

"He used to heal every miserable condition." Blathmac, a thousand years earlier, had described Christ the healer during his earthly life, gentle and caring, reaching out to all who sought him, whether they wanted healing of body or soul.

He used to go about for the good of all; he was affable, gentle in manner; in the face of any affliction he did not inflict abusive rejection or repulse.

Hearing to the deaf (pleasant occasion!), keenness to the eyes of the blind, the lepers making an exchange for a clean body, the lame walking about.

Every miserable condition that was brought to him which hand or leech could not cure – they would go home sound.

He would satisfy everyone in a gentle manner while he was curing their misery; he took no payment, demanded no fee.

It is manifest, then, that he was the Son of God whose attributes were the blameless cure of bodies and the full cure of souls.[6]

The stories of Christ's works of healing, with which Mary was frequently associated, are told in the Outer Hebrides with such a sense of immediacy that it was as though both Christ and his mother were still amongst them, walking their countryside, entering their cottages. Catherine Maclean, a crofter in Gairloch, told Alexander Carmichael what happened when Jesus and Mary were "under the wood", that is to say when they were fugitives in the Egyptian desert. They went in search of a drink of water for they were both parched with thirst in that hard, shrivelled land, and they found a dwelling, a miserable little bothy in the skirts of a glen that could have been any local dwelling. Inside they found a poor, wretched woman with a swollen breast who was nearly dying. She bared her breast and showed it to Mary, and asked her if she could do anything to help her to destroy the microbe in the pap and bring her relief.

His Mother said to Christ, "Do Thou, O Son, destroy the microbe in the pap. It is Thou Thyself, O Son of tears and sufferings, Who hast received from the Father in heaven power to perform healing on earth".

There are many things that are crossed (forbidden) and not becoming to do, and it is forbidden to a man to place his hand on a woman's breast. But Christ gave us an example in this matter, as He gave us in many another. Christ blew the warm breath of His mouth on the tortured breast, and He stretched His gentle hand thither over the pap, and He said:

Extinction to thy microbe,
Extinction to thy swelling,
Peace be to thy breast,
The peace of the King of power.

Whiteness be to thy skin,
Subsiding to thy swelling,
Wholeness to thy breast,
Fullness to thy pap.

In the holy presence of the Father,
In the holy presence of the Son,
In the holy presence of the Spirit,
The holy presence of compassion.[7]

If a woman healed a blind eye she might remind herself of the story of the time that Mary had restored the sight of a salmon. Again she would speak of it almost as if the scene, though set in the Holy Land, had actually taken place in the familiar Scottish countryside. She tells how Christ and His Mother

> were walking by the side of a river in the Holy Land. And what but it was a gentle autumn evening, the sun about to sink in the depth of the ocean, scattering gold-yellow and gold-red upon the crests of the mountains and upon the surface of the waves. And in the meeting of day and night, what but a white-bellied salmon leaped with a great rush up the rough bed of the stream. Christ noticed that the salmon was wanting the sight of an eye, and He desired the Mary Mother to give the sight of the eye back to the salmon. And the Mary Mother gave the sight of that eye back to the salmon, and the sight of that eye of the salmon was as good as that of the other eye.[8]

The woman began her own healing action by first saying the Creed of Mary (which must be the traditional Hail Mary) "with the lips of her mouth and with the cords of her heart", and placing the cross of Christ on the blind eye. She then put spittle on her own palms, and placed this on the blind eye, and in the name of the God of life, the Christ of love and the Holy Spirit, all of whom were "guiding her mind and her tongue and her eye as she searched to cure the blindness".

The healing itself therefore took place in the name of the Trinity, and indeed appeal to the Trinity was an extremely important element in the whole process of healing. A common Trinitarian blessing would be to commend the sick person

> In the eye of God,
> In the love of Jesus,
> In the name of Spirit,
> The Trinity of power.

The Trinitarian approach fitted in easily and naturally with the rhythm of performing an action three times, which was a common form of the pattern of healing. When a man or woman set about the healing of a hurt limb they would very often provide themselves with a three-plied cord or hard lint (lint was thought of as being sacred to Christ) which they would then divide into three parts of equal length. They would make a knot in the first part while breathing on it and touching it with their lips in the name of the Trinity. They repeated this with the other parts of the cord until they had done it three times with three knots. They were then ready to tie the cord round the affected limb three times, in the name of the Sacred Father, the Sacred Son and the Sacred Spirit. In the case of a sprain the injured part would be rubbed with extract from St John's wort to moisten it and to relieve the pain while a hymn to the Trinity was sung, each successive verse addressed to "the clement and kind" or to "the grace of the Three in One". Rubbing and singing proceeded together, the rubbing being done "soothingly and skilfully", as one practitioner put it, while the hymn was sung "tenderly and sympathetically".

Water collected from special wells or springs and used in healing involved certain rituals. Kate Cameron, a cottar from Kiltarlity in Inverness-shire told Alexander Carmichael, "You go with a clay crock till you reach running water over which the living and the dead cross. You must not open your mouth to person nor to animal nor to any created thing from the time you go away till the time you return home. On the lower side of the bridge on which the living and the dead go across, you shall go down on your right knee, and you shall lift a palmful of water in the hollows of your hand into the crock saying thus:

I am lifting a palmful of water
In the holy name of Father,
In the holy name of Son,
In the holy name of Spirit,
In the holy name of the Three
Everlasting, kindly, wise.

A woman crofter of Gairloch said that before she collected a basin of water from a stream in order to use it to turn back the "growth and the grip and the pain" of a cataract, she would commend what she was doing to the Trinity

Certain that They will do to me
The thing that it becomes me to ask
The thing that accords with Their mind.

She then went on to tell Carmichael how she took the water home. It is best heard in her own words:

I take the basin of water home, and three green blades of grass of the plain, and I put a piece of gold or a silver coin in the basin of water, and I dip blade after blade in the basin of water, and pray to
God the Father,
God the Son,
God the Spirit,
for guidance and compassion.
And I dip a blade of grass in the basin of water and draw the blade softly and gently across the cataract on the eyeball in the name of Father. And I dip a blade of grass in the basin of water and draw the blade softly across the cataract on the eyeball in the name of Son. And I dip a blade of grass in the basin of water and draw the blade softly and gently across the cataract on the eyeball in the name of Spirit. And I ask the everlasting Trinity of life to grant me my prayer if it be Their own will so to do and if the asking be in accord with Their mind. [9]

The healing properties of water and the role of sacred springs and wells have of course a long history within Celtic tradition. There are innumerable legends of saints conjuring up water, or enacting miracles with water. One legend can do for all the rest, since it contains the common elements found elsewhere. It is the story of how St Cadog came to Cornwall with two disciples, hot, exhausted and thirsty after their long journey, and how then finding themselves in a dry and arid place, the saint pierced the ground with his crozier

> and immediately on the spot a copious spring gushed forth from the soil, and therefrom both he and they who accompanied him all drank abundantly after the manner of the Israelitish people thirsting in the wilderness, when Moses struck the rock with a rod and waters flowed in abundance. When all were satisfied with water, he said to his companions, "Let us, brethren, earnestly entreat the divine bounty that all who come ill to this sacred fount may receive therefrom healing of divers diseases, God's grace assenting thereto, and as it quenched our raging thirst, so may it the poisonous plagues of bodies." For if any sick person drink from that fount, trusting firmly in the Lord, he will receive soundness of belly and bowels, and he will throw up in his vomit all slimy worms out of himself. After the Cornishmen had perceived that by divine pity frequent recoveries of health of both sexes were incessantly being effected at the same well, they built a little church of stone by the fountain in honour of Saint Cadog.[10]

The search for healing is a perennial search. What the Celtic world knew was the totality of healing. Body cannot be healed apart from soul, and neither can be healed apart from God. They also knew something which we all experience as children and then seem to forget: the importance of rhythm and repetition; the comfort that comes from the rhythmic touch that soothes and restores, the repetitive singing that reassures. As modern medicine turns again towards holistic medicine and herbal cures it is doing no more than turning to age-old knowledge. It is an admission of the powers that God's world holds to bring men and women into wholeness and healing. It is a gift to be treated with reverence and respect and gratitude. "Every sound man is a king." Legend tells of a conversation between St Brigit and a leper:

A leper came one time to Brigit asking for a cow. And Brigit said, "Would you sooner have a cow or be healed of your disease?"

"I would sooner be healed," he said, "than to have sway over the whole world. For every sound man is a king."[11]

the

---

light and the dark

Sin and Sorrow

"Gladly we live in this garden of your creating. . . . In the garden also: always the thorn. Creation is not enough. . . . In the garden that is each of us, always the thorn." The final lines of the three successive stanzas of George MacLeod's poem "The Whole Earth Shall Cry Glory" are saying something whose significance we should not miss. There can be no doubt about the celebration of creation, and the gratitude for the gifts of the creator. Yet the power of the Celtic lies in the ability to hold things together, to accept the forces of dark as well as the light; indeed the light without the dark will not do, the one depends on the other. It was something which Seamus Heaney actually experienced when he visited the oratory of an early hermit on a remote stretch of the coast of western Ireland, and as a poet he was able to write about it most evocatively.

"Inside, in the dark of the stone, it feels as if you are sustaining a great pressure, bowing down like the generations of monks who must have bowed down in meditation and reparation on the floor." In such a place you feel "the weight of Christianity in all its rebuking aspects, its calls to self-denial and self-abnegation, its humbling of the proud flesh and insolent spirit. But coming out of the cold heart of the stone into the sunlight and dazzle of grass and sea, I feel a lift in my heart, a surge towards happiness that must have been experienced over and over again by those monks as they crossed that same threshold centuries ago."[1]

The sense of sin, reparation for sin, extreme austerity and asceticism, all these are equally part of the Celtic way to God, and give it its power and strength as much as does its creation-centred spirituality. We are brought back once again to the Celtic cross with its powerful symbolic statement that the great circle of the world, the great O of creation, must be juxtaposed against the cross, the crucifixion; creation and redemption held together.

> Almighty God, Creator:
> The morning is Yours, rising into fullness.
> The summer is Yours, dipping into autumn.
> Eternity is Yours, dipping into time.
> The vibrant grasses, the scent of flowers, the lichen on the rocks, the tang of sea-weed.
> All are Yours.
> Gladly we live in this garden of Your creating.

> But creation is not enough.
> Always in the beauty, the foreshadowing of decay.
> The lambs frolicking careless: so soon to be led off to slaughter.
> Nature red and scarred as well as lush and green.
> In the garden also:
> always the thorn.
> Creation is not enough.

> Almighty God, Redeemer:
> The sap of life in our bones and being is Yours,
> lifting us to ecstasy.
> But always in the beauty: the tang of sin, in our consciences.
> The dry lichen of sins long dead, but seared upon our minds.
> In the garden that is each of us, always the thorn.[2]

The tang of sin, the dry lichen of sin – these are vivid images. In a tenth-century poem Eve speaks of sin, of failure, of brokenness, and does so as representative of the whole human race.

> I am Eve; great Adam's wife; it is I that outraged Jesus of old; it is I that stole heaven from my children; by rights it is I that should have gone upon the Tree.

> I had a kingly house at my command; grievous the evil choice that

disgraced me; grievous the chastisement of crime that has withered me; alas! my hand is not clean.

It is I that plucked the apple; it overcame the control of my greed; for that, women will not cease from folly as long as they live in the light of the day.

There would be no ice in any place; there would be no glistening windy winter; there would be no hell; there would be no sorrow; there would be no fear, were it not for me.[3]

The theme of human betrayal of God's love is put into the mouth of Judas in another early poem.

> Woe is me that I forsook my King;
> Evil was the deed to which I put my hand;
> Therefore shall I be for ever
> Without peace and without gentle affection.
>
> Woe to him who did it, woe to him who does it;
> Woe for his pilgrimage in this world;
> For him who is guilty of excessive covetousness,
> Woe twice over, and woe, O God.
>
> Alas, alas, the price of the betrayal of my King,
> Long, long shall I feel the evil of it;
> Thirty circles of white silver,
> 'Tis that which has tortured my body.[4]

Awareness of sin is the first step to penitence, repentance and so reparation. "Tears, O my God, who but you will give me?" Reference to tears, especially to tears of sorrow for sin, are quite common. Deep sorrow is expressed in tears. "The measure of your prayer until the tears come."[5] A twelfth-century poem asks God for the gift of tears, for "fierce floods of tears", for "a well of tears".

Grant me, O great God, in this world (I will not hide it) against the pains of the torments, fierce floods of tears.

Let a vessel unsullied reach me as it flows, so that, although all alone, I may early surmount every treacherous danger.

Alas, holy Christ, that thou bringest no stream to my cheek as thou didst bring a flood to the weak wretched woman. (Note, Mary Magdalen)

Alas that no stream reaching every part flows over my breast to be a cleansing tonight for my heart and my body.

For the sake of every venerable elder who has abandoned his inheritance, for thy glorious kingdom's sake, for the sake of thy going to the cross.

For the sake of everyone who has wept for his wrongdoing in this world, may I, O living God, bewail my wickedness.

Especially for the sake of thy goodness and for thy griefless kingdom's sake, speedily, opportunely, grant me a well of tears.[6]

The sense of sorrow and contrition was particularly strong because men and women felt that they had sinned against God in all his aspects, so in their litanies of confession, instead of the brief Roman form which is more familiar in the west, we find endless petitioning, appealing to God time and time again, asking him to hear and to forgive.

O Father, O Son, O Holy Spirit,
  Forgive me (us) my sins,
O only-begotten Son of the heavenly Father,
  Forgive. O one God, O true God, O chief God,
O God of one substance, O God only mighty, in three Persons, truly pitiful,
  Forgive.

O God above all gods, O King above all kings, O Man above men,
    Forgive.
O World above worlds, O Power above powers, O Love above loves,
O Cause above causes, O Fortress above fortresses,
O Angel above angels,
    Forgive.
Archdeacon of heaven and earth,
    Forgive. O High-Priest of all creation,
O Archbishop of the seven heavens,
    Forgive. O first Priest, O chief Priest,
O true Priest, O true Physician, O true Prophet, O true Friend,
    Forgive.
O only Sustainer of the threefold mansion, O only Life of all created
    things,
O only Light of the seven heavens,
    Forgive. O Subject of the Scriptures' meditation,
O Object of the chief prophets' search, O Father of true life,
O voice of the people,
    Forgive.[7]

Men and women do not make this journey alone. They turn for help and support to their *anamchara*, a spiritual friend or soul-friend, one who offers *anamchairdeas* or spiritual direction. This, which is peculiar to Celtic spirituality, is, as so often in the Irish Church, something that had existed before the arrival of Christianity. Every Celtic chief had his counsellor or druid at court, whose guidance he followed. The legends of St Patrick represent him as replacing Dubthach the pagan adviser to the high king Laoghaire and becoming in his place *anamchara* to the king.[8] That well-known aphorism that anyone without a soul-friend is like a body without a head is attributed both to St Brigit and to St Comgall. So important indeed was the role of the *anamchara* in monastic life that it was said that following the guidance of one's soul-friend was of more importance than subjection to a Rule.

This was not however something confined to courtly or even to monastic circles. It was quite common for lay men and women to be soul-friends. The relationships might well be between a man and a woman, between clerical and lay.

> As the members of the body diligently help one another, So let each
> show a special sign of love
> For his fellow who is in pain of soul.[9]

"Seek out him who will least spare you", says the Rule of Tallaght. "When you put yourself under the judgement or rule of another, the fire that you judge will burn you most keenly, approach it."

"Medicine for the salvation of souls." That is how the penitential of Cummaen opens. Penance was not new in the Church but Celtic practice extended it in one important direction: it made it private rather than public.

Public penance as it was practised in Europe at the time was something which tended to isolate and humiliate; penitents became the lowest of the low, excluded from the main body of the Church, charged with the fulfilling of unpleasant duties such as the carrying of corpses, and debarred for ever, for example, from returning to the married state. But now the Celtic Church made the practice of private penance much more common. Here is a cure for sin, with Christ as the physician. St Columbanus writes about it as medicine which brings about the restoration of health. "Diversity of offences causes diversity of penances. For doctors of the body also compound their medicines in diverse kinds: thus they heal wounds in one manner, sicknesses in another, boils in another, festering sores in another, eye diseases in another. So also should spiritual doctors treat with diverse kinds of cures the wounds of souls, their sicknesses, pains, ailments and infirmities. But since this gift belongs to few, namely, to know to a nicety all these things, to treat them, to restore what is weak to a complete state of health, let us set out even a few prescriptions according to the traditions of our elders, and according to our own partial understanding."[10]

Irish penitential discipline developed a system of private penance much more thoroughly than elsewhere in the contemporary Church, and when it spread from Ireland to the rest of Europe it led to the increasing frequency of confession and to a much more systematized form of private penance set out in tariffs of penance for both clergy and laity. One of the most common was the use of penitential fasting, on Wednesday and Friday, and also for more extended periods during the forty days of the three Lents: not only the usual Lent but in addition a period before Christmas and another after Pentecost. All this brought about the increasing frequency of confession, and of penance, particularly amongst the laity. St Columbanus as he travelled through Europe commented that, by contrast, in the Gallic Church of his day he found this "love of mortification" notably lacking.

The ascetical dimension of Celtic spirituality can be rather startling to the twentieth-century mind with its post-Freudian approach to life, which would tend to equate wholeness with fulfilment. But it is important to see that this Celtic asceticism is not negative, life-denying. After all, the monks from whom these penitential practices originally derived were anything but deprived and negative men; rather they were joyous and fulfilled men, at one with themselves, with the world, with God. Ascetic ideals, however, were not confined to the monasteries but spilled over into the mainstream of the Church. This is a Christianity of the laity. Irish preachers could hold up before people's eyes the prospect of penitence which would lead them to be ranked alongside the martyrs and the monks.

The Celtic understanding of martyrdom was fuller than that to which we are now accustomed.[11] It was an all-inclusive category. It is to deny ourselves, to take up our cross, to follow Christ. The whole element of suffering and renunciation in the Christian life is to be understood as a kind of martyrdom. An early eighth-century Irish text sets out the three types of martyrdom. At the heart is red martyrdom, to suffer by giving one's life for Christ, the traditional idea of dying for the faith. Next comes the white martyrdom, when a man "separates for the sake of God from everything he loves", which is the way of exile, of wandering, of *peregrinatio*. In a society that was essentially tribal and hierarchical this would also of course mean losing the security of a known place and fixed rank. Perhaps we are today in a better position to appreciate what that can mean as so many people suffer exile, loss, redundancy, displacement in all its many acute forms. There are more refugees in the world today than ever before. Vast numbers of people have been expelled from places like South Africa for following the dictates of their conscience. Exile is only too familiar to many who know that they will never return to the places and people they love. There is as well the more hidden exile, of the loss of place within society, through unemployment and early retirement, the loss of a niche within the conventional family, the loss that is known not only to the homeless, of not belonging anywhere. We could well see in all this a form of white martyrdom.

And then finally the green martyrdom, which is when a man "separates from his desires, or suffers toil in penance and repentance". This is a less spectacular vocation, it is the inner, the more hidden way. But it is a way followed by all who live a life of denial, a daily repentance for Christ's sake, the martyrdom which can be experienced by anyone without leaving home. The strength of such martyrdom, such asceticism lies not in any of the externals of fasts, vigils, mortification, but in the inner disposition of the will, bringing body and soul under control so that men and women may be set free to love and to serve God. As always this is not negative but positive. The Celtic tradition reminds us that asceticism is a profound means of spiritual growth.

Consideration of this may well make us ask if it is possible to recover any meaningful asceticism today in a culture of affluence, of instant satisfaction, consumerism, self-fulfilment. Yet already there are many signs that the world wants to draw back. This does not of course refer to those who have no such choice, the hungry for whom the possibility of voluntary fasting is non-existent, but to the average, comfortable middle-class person who is beginning to find that they are looking for restraint at many levels. This may be a more simple life-style, the training and subduing of the body, whether by jogging, dieting, health farms, or whatever the current enthusiasm is, and in particular addressing the conquering of those addictions which hold the body in thrall. Limitation, asceticism, restraint, discipline here have one end: the escape from tyranny and the movement towards freedom, so that destructive forces may be replaced by life-giving forces. Perhaps the Celtic tradition will help with the rediscovery of the role of asceticism in religious practice in its widest sense, not only at the level of fasting and penance, but by an affirming and unspectacular acceptance of the place of discipline, restraint, simplicity in daily life. The importance of the soul-friend, a spiritual guide who will help the individual to find their own path (for he or she is, in the fine phrase used by the seventeenth century Benedictine Augustine Baker, "only God's usher") is becoming more and more commonly recognized. The way of sorrow and repentance and reparation is not to be undertaken alone. Here is support so that this journey back to God, this *metanoia* of turning and returning, becomes the way to freedom and fullness of life.

Salvation

The spirituality of early Christian Ireland has a heroic character in which Jesus is the champion who delivers his people by means of a stupendous feat of physical prowess, the passion. Once again we find an outlook which puts the Christian into the same key as the saga literature of pre-Christian times. The God who delivers his people is celebrated in magnificent litanies, and in loricas, those breastplate prayers which have from the very beginning been typical of the Irish Church. The Celtic world was one in which men and women faced the reality of evil. They were willing to admit the power of the forces of darkness. They did not attempt to deny sin, pain and suffering. There was no running away here. They did not hesitate either to name the dark powers or recognize the part that they played in their lives. Today we are rarely as honest. Perhaps we are just beginning to face up to sin and evil and to talk about them. But here men and women are aware that they are caught up in a battle with the forces of evil, the dark powers, with demons. It is only through Christ himself, with all his many powers, and with the help of the angels, and the aid of the saints and the martyrs, that this battle can be fought and won. Here once again we touch on something deeply primitive, something carried from an earlier pagan past. The heathen gods too have been invoked under all their many names and through all their many powers. The most famous of these lorica prayers, St Patrick's breastplate, has been included already in this book, but it is given again here in another translation since probably nothing else conveys so powerfully this sense of the deep human need for a defence against the powers that can destroy.

I bind unto myself today
The strong name of the Trinity:
By invocation of the same,
The Three in One and One in Three.

I bind this day to me for ever
By power of faith, Christ's incarnation,
His baptism in the Jordan river,
His death on the Cross for my salvation,
His bursting from the spiced tomb,
His riding up the heavenly way,
His coming at the day of doom
I bind unto myself today!

I bind unto myself today
The power of God to hold and lead:
His eye to watch, his might to stay,
His ear to hearken to my need:
The wisdom of my God to teach,
His hand to guide, his shield to ward;
The Word of God to give me speech,
His heavenly host to be my guard!

Christ be with me, Christ within me,
Christ behind me, Christ before me,
Christ beside me, Christ to win me,
Christ to comfort and restore me,
Christ beneath me, Christ above me,
Christ in quiet, Christ in danger,
Christ in hearts of all that love me,
Christ in mouth of friend and stranger.

I bind unto myself the name,
The strong name of the Trinity:
By invocation of the same,
The Three in One and One in Three,

Of whom all nature hath creation,
Eternal father, Spirit, Word:
Praise to the Lord of my salvation –
Salvation is of Christ the Lord![1]

Prayers such as these were probably used from an early date as amulets would be and were thought of as possessing a kind of magical efficacy to ward off danger and the assaults of demons.[2] Many were produced between the eighth and the eleventh centuries by the Irish Church. This one comes from the eighth century and is attributed to St Fursa. It seeks protection for all the members of the body and commends each in turn to God's keeping.

May the yoke of the law of God be upon this shoulder,
the coming of the Holy Spirit on this head,
the sign of Christ on this forehead,
the hearing of the Holy Spirit in these ears,
the smelling of the Holy Spirit in this nose,
the vision that the people of heaven have in these eyes,
the speech of the people of heaven in this mouth,
the work of the Church of God in these hands,
the good of God and of the neighbour in these feet.
May God dwell in this heart
and this person belonging entirely to God the Father.[3]

The moment of death, the parting of body and soul, is the time when the conflict between the light and the dark intensifies. Prayers used for the commendation of the soul in extremis are also used as a general supplication. The struggle of the dark and bright angels over the departing souls was a frequent theme in early Irish homilies. It was also the first prayer in the ordinary of the mass in the Stowe Missal, written at Tallaght in the early ninth century. "We have sinned, O Lord, we have sinned, have mercy upon our sins and save us, Thou who didst guide Noah over the waves of the deluge, hearken unto us; Thou who didst call back Jonah from the abyss by a word, deliver us; Thou who didst hold out Thy hand to Peter drowning, be aiding unto us; Christ son of God, Who didst bring to pass the miracles of the Lord with our fathers, be propitious in our time, stretch forth Thy hand from on high, deliver us, O Christ. O Christ hear us, O Christ hear us, *Kyrie eleison*." Oengus, who composed a metrical martyrology at Tallaght, some time between 797 and 808, concluded it with a long litany which he described as "a city of refuge, a protection against the evil ones", and then he ended it by versifying the *commendatio animae* prayer

> Deliver me, O Jesus, as Thou didst deliver Eli and Enoch.
> Deliver me as Thou didst deliver Noah from the flood.
> Deliver me as Thou didst deliver Abraham from the hands of the Chaldeans.
> Deliver me as Thou didst deliver Lot from the sin of the cities.

In this way every sort of trouble, danger, disease can be enumerated.

> Save me, O Jesus whom Thy mother's kin rejected, as Thou didst save Jacob from his brothers' hands.
> Save me from the cause of every disease as Thou didst save Job from the devil's tribulations.

This is followed by the figures from the New Testament, Paul and Peter and John, until finally it comes to an end with the saints of recent time

> Save me as Thou didst save Patrick from the poison at Tara,
> Save me as Thou didst save Kevin from the falling of the mountain.[4]

These prayers are cries for help, an admission of human vulnerability, frailty and need, which start from a very honest acceptance of weakness and dependency upon God. This is the daily struggle which involves us all. There is nothing here of any easy-going mediocrity: instead it speaks of the cost of discipleship. Commitment to following Christ will entail this spiritual warfare. But the passion of Christ promises victory for all those who follow him, today as in the past. This brings the sense of solidarity with all those, whoever they may be, who have experienced the battle, whether they are those known through the pages of the Bible, or the saints and martyrs of more recent times. This hymn, sung every Sunday morning at the monastery of Bangor, makes particular reference to the martyrs, but since martyrdom was understood in the Celtic tradition like exile, as having a wider connotation than just the physical, those who heard it could identify with it whoever they were.

> You, Christ, are the powerful help of the martyrs
> Who entered into battle for your holy glory
> When they as victors departed from this world
> To you the saints sang Alleluia.
>
> Worthy of praise, Lord, is your wonderful power;
> Through the Holy Spirit you strengthened the martyrs,
> To crush the devil and to conquer death;
> To you the saints sing Alleluia.
>
> Guarded by the Lord's exalted hand,
> Firmly they stood against the devil,
> Always keeping wholehearted faith in the Trinity,
> To you the saints sang Alleluia![5]

So we are to draw strength from those who have fought the fight before us. This is not a Christianity to lull its followers with facile promises of an easy way: instead the promise is one of challenge, of struggle, of battle – an image which perhaps it is tempting to discard in an age whose concern is quite rightly with the finding and keeping of peace. Yet is is also no bad thing to be reminded that the spiritual life is also a battleground, that the weapons we need must be kept in good repair and that for those who stand firm there is the promise of the faithfulness of God, the God who protects his followers today as he has done in the past.

The Cross

It was common in early Christian Ireland for almost every church to have a cross near it on the outside. From the monastic rules we learn that some of the office was performed at the cross. Some psalms would be sung in the church itself and then with the singing of further hymns a procession would go to "the place of Golgotha", the cross itself, moving all the way round it. The Rule of Ailbe, in the eighth century, makes it quite clear that the community performed liturgy at the cross. "After the head monk (the abbot) to the cross with gentle choir-singing, with strong streams of tears from righteous cheeks. At the cross the head monk, the demons not shouting victory, with humility, without arguing, each confessing his sins . . ."[1] According to the first synod of St Patrick, the clergy were to ring the church bell to summon the people to prayer morning and evening, so clearly this office was not for the monks alone.

A countryside long familiar with pre-Christian standing stones and with giant prehistoric megaliths, was between the eighth and the tenth centuries to see this tradition carried forward under Christian influence into a totally new form. Great decorated high crosses began to appear in their hundreds. They can be found today in Wales, Scotland and Northumbria, but above all in Ireland, where there are still between sixty and seventy. Originally they were probably wooden processional crosses, placed within the central enclosure of a monastery. By the eighth century they began to be built in stone, standing as much as twelve or fifteen feet, sometimes even higher. Certainly nothing is more typical of the Celtic church.[2]

It is not difficult to imagine these tall crosses in outline against the skies and sunsets of Ireland or western Scotland or Northumbria. They are undoubtedly one of the supreme achievements of early Christian art. It is not simply that they are great standing stone monuments in themselves, but those which are decorated also convey a message about the Christian faith, a statement of Christian belief and understanding. Robin Flower has said that they are "sermons in stone which could be the commentary or the theme of a meditation . . . prayers in enduring stone, rising within the circuit of the monastery wall, visible at all times far and near, a perpetual silent liturgy, a dedication and a hope".[3]

The basic structure of each cross was simply that of a pyramid base carrying a rectangular shaft, with the arms set in a wheel or circle. This is the most striking and immediately arresting feature of the high cross. It has inevitably produced a great deal of academic and artistic discussion. Some scholars like to find here an expression of the transition from the pagan to the Christian world: since the druids worshipped the sun, the Celtic monks make the sign of the cross against the symbol of the sun, and this produces the wheel cross. Some see the familiar Christian symbol of the *Chi-ro* carried on into a full circle, so that it becomes the shape that has no beginning and no end, the *Alpha* and the *Omega* of the book of Revelation, the sign of resurrection and eternal life. Others claim that it has something in common with the laurel wreath which the classical world hung on the victor's standard. Yet another theory finds links with the Egyptian *ankh*, a *tau* cross with a looped top, originally a pagan symbol of life whose closeness to the Christian cross made it acceptable to Christians. Whatever its origins there is no doubt that the symbolism of the circle of creation held in tension with the cross of redemption makes a very powerful impression on anyone who today stands in front of one of these crosses.

In the earliest crosses the decoration was abstract, interlacing and interlinear spirals, a fine network of ornament such as can be seen at Ahenny or the southern cross at Castledermot. In some instances the inspiration may well have come from the techniques of metalwork, which by the eighth century were very fine indeed. The round stone bosses for example seem highly reminiscent of the enamel or glass studs used in large pieces of jewellery. Later crosses, however, are rather different for they are covered with elaborate and intricately carved panels which cover both sides of the shaft and often the underside of the arms as well. They present the story of God's work of salvation, human history from the fall to the last judgement. The scenes which the sculptors chose to illustrate have parallels in early Christian art in many other places. Representations of Noah, the sacrifice of Isaac, Daniel in the lions' den, the three children in the fiery furnace, belong to a very old tradition and can for example be found in the catacombs in Rome or in fourth- and fifth-century marble sarcophagi in Italy. The figures, and the episodes chosen, also correspond very closely to those which we have already seen in the litanies asking for the help of God: "Deliver, O Lord, thy servant as thou didst deliver thy servants in the past".[4]

In addition however to this biblical material many Irish crosses included scenes from the life of St Antony of Egypt, often placed in a dominant position in the top panel, who was taken as a model for the monastic life. Sometimes the scene will record the story which is found in St Jerome of a visit from St Paul of Thebes when a raven brought them both bread. The cross at Kells shows them seated, face to face, receiving a loaf carried down by a huge bird plunging from the skies. The raven who brings a loaf which they divide has eucharistic connotations, and some crosses even show a small chalice on the ground between them. The cross at Ruthwell in southern Scotland is accompanied by an inscription which tells us that "St Paul and St Antony hermits broke bread in the desert". Already the multi-dimensional levels at which the carvings were meant to be understood is becoming apparent. The God who saves his people also feeds them. Breaking and sharing involves sacrifice, and sacrifice is not only a common thread in many of the chosen scenes, it is also the point on which the whole cross itself depends – the central panel of the crucifixion itself.

The actual organizational plan of the panels varies from cross to cross. But there are certain fixed scenes which inevitably recur when the theme is the fall and redemption. Since, as a prayer in the mass says, the human race fell by a tree and so also was mankind redeemed by a tree, the garden of Eden is often portrayed. On the south cross at Castledermot the tree of paradise is actually in the form of a cross with six apples, and round its trunk winds the serpent whispering into Eve's ear as it hands her the apple. At Moone, and on the north cross at Castledermot, the tree has many apples and reaches right down to the ground on either side, a weeping tree which encloses the *dramatis personae* – the snake incidentally shown with a finned tail, so presumably the carver had never seen one, as St Patrick had promised! At

Moone Adam and Eve hold their hands in front of their private parts, and if it is true that these crosses were originally coloured then presumably fig leaves would have been painted here. Then follow a succession of scenes from the Old Testament, all of which may be seen to have been chosen because they show God at work rescuing fallen humanity, but also because they are seen as pre-figurations which anticipate the life of Christ. This was a way of understanding the Bible which drew its inspiration from Christ himself saying, "As Moses lifted up the serpent in the wilderness so must the Son of Man be lifted up" (St John 3.14). This was an idea developed by the early fathers, and Ireland must at this time have been familiar with it. Sometimes this unveiling of meaning, and the multiplicity of levels at which it works, can seem rather strange and subtle to a modern way of thinking. Yet once accepted it can be strangely moving. Isaac about to be sacrificed by his father is clearly an image of the sacrifice of Christ, particularly when the wood is actually in the shape of the cross. But then the meaning is extended so that it carries a further symbolism: it also speaks of God's help to his faithful people, the God of saving power who rescues his servant in the hour of need.

On one cross, that at Kells, the murder of Abel, which is placed next to the fall, shows a very tall Cain who wields a sort of hooked stick over the head of the victim, the small figure of Abel who is the prototype of Christ. Daniel on the same cross, who is seen between two lions holding out his extended arms in the form of the cross, becomes another pre-figuring of the crucifixion. The three children in the fiery furnace nestle under the wings of an angel while men pile wood on the fire with long forks, again a parallel which would be immediately obvious to contemporaries since the figure of Christ on the cross was always at this time represented with a figure on either side, one with the long lance, the other with a bowl of vinegar at the end of a long pole. Of the New Testament scenes the flight into Egypt is quite often chosen since it not only shows God rescuing his people but also keeps up the theme of the desert. At Moone Mary is depicted sitting side-saddle with only the child's head visible, protected and encircled by the mother; directly opposite are two scenes from monastic Egypt, so that it suggests a pre-figuring of the later desert. Underneath this comes the feeding of the five thousand, shown simply with five loaves and two fishes artistically arranged. A great sense of decoration comes from the fact that the large fish are in fact Egyptian mouth-breeding cichlids (a nice reminder of the connection with the East since these are fish not known in western seas), whose elegant circular shapes harmonize well with the round loaves. This of course also brings back the theme of the eucharist, the breaking and the sharing which makes possible the feeding.

The pyramidical base of the cross at Moone, which is the foundation of the rest of the structure, shows the twelve, and at the same time would bring to mind the passage in Revelation, "the city walls stood on twelve foundation stones, each one of which have the name of one of the twelve apostles of the Lamb" (21.14). Even though they are literally the twelve apostles they must also symbolize the community of the saved, they are the twelve leaders of the new Israel, in other words they represent the Church, the people redeemed by the blood of Christ – and hence all of us. We can study, criticize and assess, but in the end we must also allow ourselves to be involved, allow these scenes to reach the feelings, address the heart. This is our story too, the salvation which God makes available to each one of us. These great high crosses stand as a public proclamation of the faith, crying aloud their message: God helps his faithful, God rescues his people from death and oppression. Here is the hope and the promise of those prayers: "Save us O Lord as thou didst save thy people in the past . . . Deliver us O Lord from all danger . . ."

All these successions of panels converge on the two central scenes, the crucifixion and the last judgement. There is probably no finer representation of the last judgement than that on the cross of Muirdeach at Monasterboice. We see a large figure of Christ who holds a cross and a flowering bough, symbol of the resurrection. He is surrounded by various different figures: one playing a harp, another a reedpipe, a third a trumpet, and another holding a book. Behind them the elect, a tightly packed crowd in three rows, look towards the figure of Christ, while the damned on his left look away as they are driven from his sight by two devils, one armed with a particularly large fork, the other who has a book is giving them a kick. Below Christ's feet St Michael holds the scales with which he is weighing a small human person and at the same time fending off with a lance or a crozier the attempt of a small devil to pull on the scales. It is an animated scene, full of life. It also shows once again Egyptian influences. The weighing of souls probably passed from the Egyptian Book of the Dead and was adapted by Coptic artists to Christian use and spread to Asia Minor and Armenia and so to Ireland where it fitted in well with the interest found in speculation about doomsday and the other-world of Irish literature. The sprouting bough and the cross are reminiscent of staffs held by Osiris-Judge in Egyptian funerary carvings and in fact the figure of Christ as judge in Osirian attitude is unique.

The impression that the scene of the crucifixion makes is one of intense suffering. On either side of Christ stand two men, Longinus who is carrying a lance which he is thrusting into Christ's side, and Stephaton who is offering him a cup of vinegar at the end of a long pole. This in addition of course gives it a pleasing symmetrical artistic balance. Here the Irish sculptors are following a tradition well established by this time, an arrangement found for example in sixth-century Syrian gospels. It also establishes the non-historical character of the scene since these two actions were separate in time, the one taking place before Christ had died, and the other after. It is also an attempt to universalize the message of the Church. Longinus who was traditionally supposed to have had his blindness cured by the water and the blood pouring from the wounded side, is taken to be the figure of the Church; Stephaton, bearer of the bitter drink, of the synagogue. The tender figures of Mary or of St John are never shown, and in only one or two cases, a rare unbending on the part of the sculptor, do angels appear to support the head of Christ. Sometimes the outstretched hands are immense, totally out of proportion to the rest – they have become the Hand of God held out towards the world, reaching out to save and to feed all his people. And again sometimes Christ is shown wearing a long robe. This makes him at once the suffering and dying Christ and also the resurrected Christ, the risen Lord of Easter. It shows once again the Celtic ability to hold two things in tension: death and life brought together.

"I bitterly lament Christ being crucified." When Blathmac, in his long poem written around the mid eighth century, came to his account of the crucifixion, he described it with a sense of vivid immediacy, as though telling of what he himself had witnessed. He is no detached spectator who watches as from a distance; he is standing there engaged, caught up in the spectacle of that pain and suffering. "Alas, for anyone who has seen the Son of the living God stretched fast on the cross! alas, the body possessing wisest dignity that has plunged into gore!"

Your people seized your son; Mary, they flogged him. There struck him the green reed and fists across ruddy cheeks.

It was a hideous deed that was done to him; that his very mother-kin should crucify the man who had come to save them.

Hands were laid upon the face of the King who was severely chastised. Hideous deed! – the face of the Creator was spat upon.

When every outrage was committed against him, when capture was completed, he took his cross upon his back – he did not cease being beaten.

When his cross was placed between the two crosses of the condemned ones he was raised (alas!) upon the cross; it was very painful.

A crown of thorns was placed (this was severe excess) about his beautiful head; nails were driven through his feet, others through his hands.

A purple cloak was put about the King by the ignoble assembly; in mockery that was put about him, not from a desire to cover him.

They tore from him his pure raiment; beautiful was the body that they stripped; lots were cast without any deception to see who might take his blessed spoils.

When they thought thus that Jesus could be approached, Longinus then came to slay him with the spear.

The King of the seven holy heavens, when his heart was pierced, wine was spilled upon the pathways, the blood of Christ flowing through his gleaming sides.

They presented him with a parting drink; through eagerness for his speedy death; they mix (illicit deed!) gall for him with vinegar.

He raises a beautiful protesting voice beseeching his holy Father: "Why have you abandoned me, living God, to servitude and distress?"[5]

The tenderness and the pain are caught in this short early poem.

At the cry of the first bird
They began to crucify Thee,
O cheek like a swan.
It were not right ever to cease lamenting –
It was like the parting of the day from night,
Ah! though sore the suffering
Put upon the body of Mary's Son –
Sorer to Him was the brief
That was upon her for His sake.[6]

"Mary's vision" is the fore-telling of Christ's death in a conversation in which she explains why she cannot sleep and tells her dream. Douglas Hyde said that there was no part of Ireland in which this was not to be found. People knew it by heart and would say it three times before going to sleep at night.

Are you asleep, Mother?
    I am not, indeed, my son.
How is that, Mother?
    Because of a vision I have of thee.
What vision is that, Mother?
    There came slim dark man on a slender black steed,
    A sharp lance in his left hand,
    Which pierceth thy right hand side.
    Letting thy sacred blood pour down upon thee.
True is that vision, Mother.[7]

The actual details, in particular the description of Christ's sufferings, will vary from place to place. This comes from Aran.

Because the Son of God is being scourged, being punished,
With narrow ropes of hemp to posts of stone,
The spear of venom going through His side,
The crown of thorns going through His head,
Blunt nails going into His feet,
His share of blessed blood being poured on the stone of the street.[8]

The passion of Christ is the cornerstone of their faith and the hope of the people who gave Douglas Hyde these verse prayers as he travelled the length and breadth of Ireland. This one comes from Philip Waldron of Drombaun near Ballyhaunis in County Mayo:

A hundred welcomes to Thee, O Blessed Body,
A hundred welcomes to Thy Body that was crucified.
A hundred welcomes to Thy Body, O Lord.
O Son of God, to Thee all hail,
O Tree, whose blossoms never fail,
Thy Boughs of luck perfume the gale
As Mark and Matthew both have told us.
If Thou art willing to accept us
And hold us in thy hand as precious
Mercy I ask of Thee and grace
For me and for each who of Adam's race is
Whom God and the Church have bade us pray for. Amen[9]

Here is this humble, hopeful cry

Weakly I go from the load within
Deeply repenting with woe my sin.
I acknowledge the faith of my God this day
With love from my heart and hope alway.
From the foot of Thy cross I call to Thee
O Jesus Lord, bow down to me.[10]

"Remember (or think of) the cross each day." Hyde gives a poem which was probably medieval but handed down from age to age, "And the King of the Graces who was raised upon it, Think upon that and on His passion . . ." So it runs in literal translation.

Making the sign of the cross was the most immediate way of asking for the protection of God. Monks and hermits would pray the cross vigil, holding out their arms in lengthy prayers. But ordinary people would simply make the sign of the cross over even the most humble of daily activities to ward off evil and commend themselves and their activity to God. This would come very naturally to people living in a world in which they felt that the forces of light and dark were always close at hand. Adomnan in his biography of St Columba just mentions in passing that unless a milk pail in Iona was marked with the sign of the cross before it was filled a demon might leap in and hide under the milk. It is therefore hardly surprising to find the many short blessings and invocations that were passed down in oral tradition keep alive this sense of the need to involve God's help in ordinary daily life. Douglas Hyde said that in later nineteenth-century Ireland it was the custom when any sudden trouble came upon men and women to exclaim, "the Cross of Christ upon us". People still believed that there was an invisible host around them, ready to hurt them if it had the chance. So they would use the cross as one would use a weapon.

> May it be a strong fortress, the fortress in which we are,
> May it be a blind host, this host that is coming to us.[11]

When danger and uncertainty were ever-present realities the necessity of the shielding of God became equally important. In Scotland prayers for protection were often accompanied by the ritual of encompassment or "caim". Anyone in fear or danger or distress would make an imaginary circle by stretching out the right hand with the forefinger extended, and then turning in the direction of the sun they would draw this circle around themselves to enclose and accompany them and safeguard them from all evil, whether internal or external.

The compassing of God and His right hand
Be upon my form and upon my frame;
The compassing of the High King and the grace of the Trinity
Be upon me abiding ever eternally,
Be upon me abiding ever eternally.

May the compassing of the Three shield me in my means,
The compassing of the Three shield me this day,
The compassing of the Three shield me this night,
From hate, from harm, from act, from ill.[12]

Many of these invocations from the Carmina Gadelica have much the
same character as the earlier loricas, not least in their sense of the
totality of the presence of God surrounding each person.

The Three Who are over me,
The Three Who are below me,
The Three Who are above me here,
The Three Who are above me yonder,
The Three Who are in the earth,
The Three Who are in the air,
The Three Who are in the heaven,
The Three Who are in the great pouring sea.[13]

The need is for support and protection not only from visible but also
invisible danger, the inner as well as the exterior.

May God free me from every wickedness,
May God free me from every entrapment,
May God free me from every gully,
From every tortuous road, from every slough.

May God open to me every pass,
Christ open to me every narrow way,
Each soul of holy man and woman in heaven
Be preparing for me my pathway.[14]

Hyde found many short verses on the cross which were in common usage. This one is a prayer addressed to the Christ who is the King of the wounds.

O King of the Wounds
Who wast crucified on the tree,
Thy breast and Thy side
The Blind One so pierced on Thee
That the Blood from Thy side
Was a curdling tide to see
Oh, under Thy wing
To paradise bring Thou me.[15]

The woman who gave him this short poem told him that it came from Connemara.

O Lord who didst suffer Thy tortures for me,
Torn with iron from the head to the knee,
Whose feet and whose hands were nailed to the tree,
Help, Lord! I come seeking protection of Thee.

Another from a man in the west of county Mayo:

From the foot of the Cross I look up to Thee
O Jesus Lord bow down to me.
For I stand in the faith of my God today
Put love in my heart and hope alway.[16]

Finally these lines from Aran: "Tree straight, leafy, green, beneath whose feet Christ was crucified, we return to Thee again O Cross, we return to thee again with joy."

A World Made Whole

God is at work making his world whole. That, finally, is what we gain from a re-discovery of the Celtic tradition. The inter-relationship and the inter-connectedness of all things has been an underlying theme of this book. Everything, all those dualities of heart and mind, of time and eternity, of East and West, of pagan and Christian, of the inner and the outer all come under the sway of a creator God whose all-inclusive love allows everything the freedom to be itself and yet also brings all together into one whole. A world made whole; a world in which the divides go down, and the barriers are crossed, becomes a world which integrates and heals. This is not a matter of philosophical speculation: it is something which is lived out – for the most part totally un-selfconsciously. The barriers between this world and the next simply fall away naturally. A seventh-century saint can walk and talk with angels; a twentieth-century Welsh poet finds no boundary line between the two dimensions:

There is no barrier between two worlds in the Church,
The Church militant on earth
Is one with the Church triumphant in heaven,
And the saints are in this Church which is two in one.
They come to worship with us, our small congregation,
The saints our oldest ancestors . . .

Later in this poem Gwenallt describes how Dewi, St David, told people of God's natural order as he travelled through the land like a gypsy with the altar and the Gospel in his caravan, going to the colleges and schools, pits and factories, and ordinary homes. There he

Put the holy vessels on the kitchen table
With bread from the pantry and wine from the cellar, And
He stood behind the table like a tramp
So as not to hide from us the wonder of the sacrifice.
And after Communion we had a talk round the fire
And he spoke to us of God's natural order. . . .[1]

The medieval Welsh poet Dafydd ap Gwilym sees the natural things
that he finds in the woods, the river mist, the leaf, the mayflower,
birdsong, as furnishing the eucharist in the church – the censer smoke,
a holy wafer; the lace surplice, the choir.

A pleasant place I was at today
Under the mantles of the worthy green hazel, . . .
I heard, in polished language,
A long and faultless chanting,
An unhesitant reading to the people
Of a Gospel without mumbling;
The elevation, on the hill for us there,
Of a good leaf for a holy wafer.[2]

A contemporary Welsh poet Euros Bowen looks outward from the
church into the wood, through the clear glass, and finds a common
source in the gifts of God's created world, and the gifts laid on the altar.

The reredos
Was not a decorative work of art
Full of Church symbols,
But clear glass
With the danger
Of drawing our attention
Away from the things that are proper to the communion table.

For in the transparency
The green blueness of the earth
Was branching in the sight of the morning,
The flowing of the river was a blossoming,

The sky was a joyous flight. And the sunlight
Enflamed the clouds.

And I noticed
The priest's eyes
As if he were unknowingly
Putting his hands
On these gifts,
As if these gifts of nature,
Were
The bread and the wine.[3]

The restoration of all things in Christ begins in the mystery of the eucharist. Here it takes place in a small hillside church in Wales. There is nothing very spectacular about such a building, it is part of the landscape, it grows out of the local wood and stone and earth. Perhaps a church like this is not so very different from those simple stone barnlike churches or those beehive-shaped stone oratories of early Ireland or early Northumbria. Here in all these places Christ is celebrated, the centre of the universe, the keystone in the structure which God designed. It is as though the entire universe is simply one whole in which past and present, earth and heaven, are embraced. There is no division into two realms, the natural and the supernatural, but the two flow together into one, "The mutual enclosure of this world in the next and the next in this", in the words of Charles Williams.[4]

Angels of course belong easily and naturally in both worlds, and move with peculiar ease between the two. In the Celtic world they never appear as remote or disembodied beings; instead they are thoroughly approachable and kindly. There are many accounts of the early saints spending time in their company. "Coemgen crossed the summits with the angel" says the life of St Kevin, describing that road which runs through the Wicklow gap to Glendalough. Certain places within the monastic enclosure at Iona "were frequented with angels at that time" wrote Adomnan in his biography of St Columba, and St Finnio going to meet him exclaimed, "Look, behold now the holy Columba comes, who has deserved to have as his travelling-companion an angel of heaven." Angels might surround the saints from the moment of their birth. It was said of St Brendan of Clonfort that when he was born there was a great blaze of light, and "an attendance of angels in shining white garments all round", and when he was given to his foster-mother Ita she loved him exceedingly "because she saw the attendance of angels above him, and the grace of the Holy Spirit evidently abiding on him". He was always smiling at the nun whenever he saw her and one day she asked him what it was that pleased him. "Thou," he replied, "I see thee talking to me continually, and numberless other virgins like thee, nurturing me in turn", and these of course were really angels.[5]

St Columba said that he loved Derry "because it is full of white angels from one end to the other".[6] It was not at all uncommon for them to be seen as they slipped in and out of certain places. St Brendan kneeling in a church watched a bright angel who came in by a window and lighted all the candles in the church and then went out by the window again to heaven. The monks at Iona spying on St Columba as he prayed on a certain small hill, his hands outstretched to the sky and his eyes raised to heaven, saw "holy angels, citizens of the heavenly country", all clothed in white raiment, who flew down with marvellous suddenness, and began to stand around him and after talking with him returned to heaven. Some saints were already in effect dwelling amongst the angels. A story is told of Cainnech, friend of St Columba, and of how they were both with Comgall when it began to rain, yet Cainnech remained dry. The others asked him why this should be, and he in turn asked them what they were thinking of. St Columba replied that he was thinking of his monks in peril on the sea, and Comgall said of the harvest. Whereupon Cainnech then told them, "The son of the Virgin knows that my mind is in heaven among the angels from the day I first turned it there, and I have never turned my attention to worldly things."

Angels are of course particularly associated with help on journeys. "Henceforth I will be ever with thee," said St Brendan's angel at the outset of his travels, and on the voyage itself brought all sorts of provisions and loaded the ship. When Abban set out over the sea angels were clearly seen on either side of him, and when he was on land, and night fell and it was cold and dark and he and his companions could not move a step on the way, an angel came to meet them with a bright taper to guide them until they reached their own monastery.[7]

For angels are in fact intensely practical and useful. When St Columba spent time at Clonard under St Finnian, and each man used to grind the quern in turn, an angel used to grind on behalf of St Columba. The same story is told of St Ciaran at Clonmacnois, that when he had to take his turn at grinding the angels would do it on the day that was his. When Mochuda's monks complained that their fields were ripe but they had no reapers for the harvest he replied, "God is able to give you reapers," and a band of angels immediately descended on the fields and did the reaping. And when the monks of Colmain were disappointed in being unable to attend the fair at Telltown the angels came and ran races for them.[8]

So angels were not above being involved in ordinary things if they were needed. Saints and angels are ready at hand, as we have seen in an earlier chapter, to give help in the daily lives of humble men and women. Men and women in fact knew very well that they were surrounded by angels here and now, even when they also looked forward to the promise that in God's royal hall in heaven they would be part of a merry community there. Heaven was quite commonly talked about with a sense of familiarity. Douglas Hyde collected this very simple little poem from an old blind piper in Roscommon. In literal translation is reads: "If I were in heaven would it not be fine, my story! or amongst the apostles, the angels and the saints, giving praise and thanks to the one Son of God, and the glory of the Heaven . . . We shall see Peter and we shall see Paul, we shall see Mark and we shall see John, we shall see the apostles and the angels in plenty . . ."[9]

How does one reach the Promised Land? That is the perennial question. St Brendan set out to find it in one of the most famous sea voyages of all time, and it is possible to read about that voyage as a voyage of adventure and fantasy. But it is also the story of a monk who was discovering the interplay between the temporal and the eternal, learning about the places, and above all the times, of this world, and the tension that they reveal with divine reality. He journeys from community to community keeping the liturgical year and the divine office, and the whole dramatic structure unfolds around two key anchor points, the Easter cycle and the Christmas cycle. So this is not simply an exploration of exotic lands and strange places, but of the attempt to live, move and respond to the world out of a "transfigured centre".[10]

If life centres on the Trinity that never appears as a cold, remote mystery. The frequent telling of the story of the shamrock may have blunted some of the awareness of its significance. St Patrick bends down and holds up a common plant, and so presents to his people a truth that is to be received not only as an act of intellectual assent but as an act of love. The Trinity thus becomes something close at hand, to be known and accepted in all simplicity. Of course the majesty of the Trinity is to be invoked in all its fullness and power, and St Patrick does it himself on the hill of Slane, on that Holy Saturday when his kindling of the Easter fire brought down upon him and his followers the wrath of the high King of Tara. Then, in their hour of most desperate need, he and his monks turned to the Trinity.

> At Tarah today, in this awful hour,
> I call on the Holy Trinity!

There is no invocation of the Trinity greater than this. But at the same time the sense of familiarity is never lost – the Trinity is acclaimed in "friendliness and love". A seventeenth-century Welsh writer finds the presence of the Trinity something entirely natural. "The Trinity abides with us exactly the same as the ore in the earth, or a man in his house, or a child in the womb, or a fire in a stove, or the sea in a well or as the soul is in the eye."[11] Some verses collected at the end of the last century in Ireland by Eleanor Hull run

> Three folds of the cloth, yet only one napkin is there,
> Three joints in the finger, but still only one finger fair;
> Three leaves of the shamrock, yet no more than one shamrock to wear,
> Frost, snow-flakes and ice, all in water their origin share,
> Three Persons in God; to one God alone we make prayer.[12]

A God who is Trinity in unity would seem familiar to a people for whom the tribe, the household, the family were the most immediate reality of their lives. A rural world without large towns but ruled by kings who were close to their subjects, often indeed related as kin, brings with it a certain approach to religion. It is essentially an appreciation of what relationship means. It will involve not only the members of the family or the kingdom, but extends outward to include all beings, the wild creatures, the elements, the whole universe. Nothing exists in isolation. David Jones once said that the favourite phrase for any artist must be that of psalm 122 where Jerusalem is described as a city "at unity in itself", and he added that in Welsh that word translates as interjoining, the crafting between the whole and the parts.[13] There is order and harmony in the universe as the Celtic world saw it, a unitive simplicity which finds echoes in native American spirituality or in African traditional religion. Towards the end of that marvellous book *The Primal Vision. Christian Presence Amid African Religion* John V. Taylor writes: "The primal vision is of a world of presences, of face to face meeting not only with the living, but just as vividly with the dead and with the whole totality of nature."[14] Here is life seen in its wholeness – and it is something that most people in the West today have forgotten, and are beginning to search for again. It is not impossible to find, though it asks for sensitivity and for time. I believe that the gift of the Celtic world is to renew that lost vision.

I find images of what it can mean in the artifacts which the Celtic world has left us, and it is with two of these that I want to draw this book to its end. "Wonder upon wonder" – Giraldus Cambrensis the twelfth-century Welsh traveller had stood in awe at his first sight of the Book of Kells. He felt himself caught up in the beauty and intricacy of its design. The longer he gazed at it the more he felt himself drawn into its depths and the more he came to see what was in it. In many ways it can still tell us a great deal about the Celtic world, about its originality and its power. For here is a superb example of their genius in the art of holding things together. Lines and figures and decoration are brought into a living relationship of extraordinary beauty and richness. Minute and intricate detail plays its part in making a coherent and unified whole. The monk who was responsible for the opening of St John's Gospel (for it is now recognized that the book is by a number of different hands) works with quite amazing delicacy as he winds spirals with a thread that almost becomes invisible and keeps the interconnecting lines going without ever blundering, however microscopic the interlacings may be. He brings into his canvas all the familiar figures, the vines and the spirals, the elongated animals and birds, and in particular his favourite ribbon-shaped snakes. With all of these he endlessly explores form and pattern. Yet with all his care for detail he never loses sight of his ultimate purpose and in spite of its intricacy his work is never confused. He does not aim at symmetry though he does care about coherence. This means that he will seldom balance two equal motifs exactly, and even though he may start to draw in identical patterns he will destroy the similarity by some irregular arrangement of his colours or by the sudden alteration of a few curves, by the use of unexpected and hidden rhythms. He manages to exercise a subtle sense of control over this realm of creative fantasy, so that the final impression which his illumination brings is that of order and composure. The entire Book of Kells shows this same inspired ability to use elements from varying sources and weld them together into a harmonious unity.[15]

The sophisticated handling of decoration clearly owes much to the brilliant La Tène work of the earlier Celts, for there is still present the persistent memory of ancient Celtic art, not least in the frequent use of the spiral, a common pagan motif. But there is also an open and eager readiness to use Christian continental and eastern elements, so that this native genius is here married to the Coptic and the Byzantine. Much in the Book of Kells takes us back to oriental prototypes. "Chief treasure of the Western world" the annals of Ulster were proud to proclaim it around the year 1000.

The Ardagh chalice is another such treasure. The immediate impression that it gives is of delicacy of workmanship and extraordinary beauty. It comes from a tradition of Irish metalwork which at that time held unparalleled mastery in the Christian world of the west.[16] Its decoration is a fine design, owing something in its use of strips of glass plaques to continental jewellery but ultimately it remains simply the achievement of an artist who can use filigree work and enamel with such control that he brings to it an overall sense of consummate harmony. There is a feeling here of freedom, of colour and invention and experimentation of form, and yet in the end we are left with a sense of unity. Everything is held together by an instinct for relationship and rhythm. Perhaps the complicated internal rhyme of the early Irish lyrics shows this same sort of genius. However that may be explained, it still remains a useful image at the end of this final chapter for the superb achievement by which it holds things together and brings them into a harmonious relationship.

Notes

PREFACE

1. 'Celtic Spirituality', Gordon S. Wakefield ed. *A Dictionary of Christian Spirituality*, SCM, 1983, pp. 83–4.
2. *Carmina Gadelica, Hymns and Incantations, with Illustrative Notes of Words, Rites and Customs Dying and Obsolete:* Orally Collected in the Highlands and Island of Scotland by Alexander Carmichael, 6 volumes published by the Scottish Academic Press, between 1900 and 1954. See also *The Celtic Vision, Selections from the Carmina Gadelica* ed. Esther de Waal, Darton, Longman & Todd, 1988.
3. Douglas Hyde, *Religious Songs of Connacht*, London, Dublin, 1906, II, republished with an introduction by Dominic Daly, Irish University Press, Shannon, Ireland, 1972.
4. John Taylor, *The Primal Vision, Christian Presence Amid African Religion*, SCM, 1963, pp. 196–7.
5. Kuno Meyer trans. *Selections from Ancient Irish Poetry*, Constable, 1911, pp. 25–7.

GOD'S WORLD

1. *Carmina Gadelica* I pp. 62–3.
2. Douglas Hyde, *Religious Songs* II p. 207.
3. *Carmina Gadelica I p. 231. Celtic Vision* p. 74.
4. *Carmina Gadelica* I pp. 234-5, *Celtic Vision* p. 77.
5. Hyde, II p. 47.
6. This comment comes from Dominic Daly in his introduction to the new edition of Douglas Hyde, *Religious Songs of Connacht*, Irish University Press, 1972.
7. Hyde, II p. 385.

8. An tath uinseann O.C.S.O., *Urnaithe Na Ngael, Traditional Irish Prayers*, 1976, pp. 13–15.

9. Saltain, *Prayers from The Irish Tradition*, Columba Press, Dublin, 1988, p. 12.

10. *Carmina Gadelica* I pp. 270–1, *Celtic Vision* p. 83.

11. *Carmina Gadelica* IV pp. 64–5, *Celtic Vision* p. 79.

12. *Carmina Gadelica* IV p. 87. *Celtic Vision* p. 84.

13. Whitley Stokes ed., *Lives of the Saints* from *Book of Lismore*, Oxford, 1890, pp. 186–7.

14. Peig Sayers, *An Old Woman's Reflections* trans. Seamus Ennis, Oxford, 1962. This comes from the introduction by W. R. Rodgers p. xii.

15. *Celtic Vision* p. 72 and p. 85.

16. *Carmina Gadelica* III pp. 180–1. It is set out in full in *Celtic Vision* p. 145.

17. *Carmina Gadelica* III p. 49, *Celtic Vision* p. 145.

18. *Carmina Gadelica* I pp. 272–3.

19. *Carmina Gadelica* IV p. 41, *Celtic Vision* p. 57.

20. *Carmina Gadelica* I pp. 246–7, *Celtic Vision* p. 53.

21. *Celtic Vision* p. 111.

22. *Carmina Gadelica* III pp. 17–19, *Celtic Vision* pp. 115–6.

23. *Carmina Gadelica* III p. 247, *Celtic Vision* p. 139.

24. *Carmina Gadelica* II p. 83, *Celtic Vision* p. 99.

25. Hyde, II, p. 369.

26. E. Hull, *Poem Book of the Gael*, Chatto, 1912 p. xxxvii.

MONKS AND HERMITS

1. See pp. 67–8.

2. John T. McNeill, *The Celtic Churches. A History AD 200 to 1200*, University of Chicago Press, 1974, p. 70.

3. R. W. D. Finn, "The Age of The Saints", David Walter ed. *History of The Church in Wales*.

4. K. H. Jackson, *A Celtic Miscellany*, Routledge and Kegan Paul, 1951, p. 148.

5. Kathleen Hughes and Ann Hamlin, *Celtic Monasticism: The Modern Traveller to the early Irish church*, Seabury Press, New York, p. 1.

6. Jackson, *Celtic Miscellany*, pp. 312–13, shortened.

7. N. K. Chadwick, *The Age of the Saints in the Early Celtic Church.* Oxford University Press, 1961, pp. 157–8. This remains the most scholarly and sympathetic study of Celtic Christianity.

8. Hughes, *Celtic Monasticism*, p. 12.

9. Julia Smith "Celtic asceticism and Carolingian authority in early medieval Brittany", W. J. Shields ed. *Monks, Hermits and the Ascetic Tradition*, Studies in Church History, Blackwell, 1985, vol. 22, p. 59.

10. Stokes. *Lives of Saints from the Book of Lismore*, pp. 168–9.

11. J. N. Hillgarth "The East, Visigothic Spain and the Irish", *Studia Patristica*, IV, 2, Oxford Patristic Congress 1969, pp. 442–56. Also Joseph H. Crehan, "The Liturgical Trade Route: East to West", *Studies*, Dublin, 1976, LXV, pp. 87–99.

12. G. V. Murphy "The Place of John Eriguena in the Irish learning tradition", p. 101 and Martin McNamara "The psalter in early Irish monastic spirituality", *Monastic Studies*, Advent, 1983, 14, p. 201.

13. Geraldine Carvelle, "The Road from Camus to Moone – An Expression of Celtic Monasticism", *ibid.*, p. 176.

14. Chadwick, *The Age of the Saints*, p. 60.

15. John Ryan, *Irish Monasticism, Origins and Early Development*, Longmans, 1931, p. 222. This remains the classic study of the subject.

16. A. W. Wade-Evans, *Vitae Sanctorum Britanniae et Genealogiae*, University of Wales, Cardiff, 1944, p. 177. See also, on the subject of Welsh saints, Elissa R. Henken, *Traditions of the Welsh Saints*, D. S. Brewer, 1987 and G. H. Doble, ed. D. Simon Evans, *Lives of the Welsh Saints*, University of Wales, Cardiff, 1971.

17. C. Plummer, *Lives of the Irish Saints*, Oxford, 1922, II, p. 153.

18. Daphne D. C. Pochin Mould, *The Irish Saints*, Dublin, 1964, p. 218.

19. Wade-Evans, *Vitae Sanctorum* p. 203.

20. *Ibid.*, see pp. 194–234.

21. G. S. M. Walker trans. and ed., *Sancti Columbani opera*, Epist. 4:4, Dublin, 1957, pp. 28–9.

22. Sr Benedicta Ward, SLG, "St. Cuthbert, The Lives and the Early Church", G. Bonner, David Rollason and Clare Stancliffe eds, *St Cuthbert, His Cult and His Community to AD 1200*, The Boydell Press, 1989, pp. 39ff.

23. Pochin Mould, *Irish Saints*, p. 60.

24. James Coutts, "The True Desert is Oneself", introduction to the Welsh Background of the Hermit Life, *Celtic Theology*, S.C.M. pamphlet no. 33 p. 19.

25. *Vitae Sancti Hiberniae*, II, 50, quoted Peter O'Dwyer, *Celi De*, Carmelite Publications, Dublin, 1981, p. 171.

26. Eoin de Bhaldraithe "Irish Monastic Rules", *Hallel*, A *Review of Monastic Spirituality and Liturgy*, 1987, 15, 1, pp. 47–92.

27. Anderson, Allan Orr and Marjorie Ogilvy trans and eds, *Adomnan's Life of Columba*, Nelson, 1961, pp. 523–9.

PILGRIMS AND EXILES

1. Sermon 8, quoted Pochin Mould, *Irish Saints* p. 105.

2. F. S. M. Walker, "St Columbanus: monk or missionary?", G. J. Cuming ed. *The Mission of the Church and the Propagation of the Faith*, Studies in Church History, 1970, vol. 6, pp. 39–45.

3. See Eleanor Duckett *The Wandering Saints*, Collins, 1959, and William H. Marnell *Light from the West. The Irish Mission and the Emergence of Modern Europe*, Seabury Press, New York, 1978. These are the two best studies of the subject.

4. Thomas Merton, "From Pilgrimage to Crusade", *Cithora*. St Bonaventure, New York, 1964, p. 5 quoted Patrick Hart, "The Heritage of Celtic Monasticism", *Cistercian Studies*, I. 1966:1, pp. 39–54.

5. Gerard Murphy, ed. *Early Irish Lyrics, Eighth to Twelfth Century*, Oxford, 1956, p. 19.

6. Duckett, *The Wandering Saints*, p. 24.

7. Kuno Meyer, *Ancient Irish Poetry*, p. 100. *Palaeohibernicus*, II, 296.

8. Chadwick, *The Age of The Saints*, p. 83.

9. Stokes, *Lives of Saints from The Book of Lismore*, p. 259.

10. Meyer, *Ancient Irish Poetry*.

11. Duckett, *The Wandering Saints*, p. 26.

12. James Carney, *Early Irish Poetry*, Mercier Press, Cork, 1965, pp. 15–16.

13. *Ibid.*, p. 35.

14. Marnell, *Light from the West*, p. 1.

15. Kathleen Hughes. "An Irish Litany of Pilgrim Saints, compiled c. 800", *Analecta Bollandia*, 1959, 77, p. 321.

16. John Hennig, "Irish Saints in the Literary and Artistic Tradition of Central Europe", *Irish Ecclesiastical Record*, 1943, 61, pp. 181–202.

17. E. G. Bowen, *Saints, Seaways and Settlements in the Celtic Lands*, University of Wales, Cardiff, 1977, p. 69.

18. For St Columbanus in addition to works already referred to on page 143, note 21, and note 2 above, see Duckett *Wandering Saints* pp. 118–40 and Marnell, *Light from the West* pp. 77–100. There is a full criticial bibliographical note in Marnell pp. 100–2. Also see Jean Le Clercq "The Religious Universe of St Columbanus", *Aspects of Monasticism*, Cistercian Publications 1978, pp. 187–207.

19. Letter to the bishops of Gaul, G. S. M. Walker *Scriptures Latini Hiberniae*, 2, Dublin, 1958, pp. 16–17.

20. Pochin Mould, *The Irish Saints*, p. 118.

21. See Cynthia Bourgeault. "Navigation of St Brendan", *Monastic Studies*, 14, pp. 109–22. For the historical St Brendan see Pochin Mould, *The Irish Saints*, pp. 36–41. The text itself will be found in Plummer, *Lives of Irish Saints*, II, pp. 44–93.

22. *Adomnan's Life of Columba* p. 321.

23. *Ibid.*, p. 223.

24. *Ibid.*, pp. 445–7.

25. Bowen, *Saints, Seaways and Settlements* p. 78.

26. Kathleen Hughes, "An Irish Litany of Pilgrim Saints compiled c. 800" *Analecta Bollandia*, 1959, 77. pp. 305–37.

27. Plummer, *Lives of Irish Saints*, II, pp. 301–2.

THE UNIVERSE

1. Noel Dermot O'Donoghue, *Aristocracy of Soul, Patrick of Ireland*, Darton, Longman & Todd, 1987. The appendix contains *The Confession*. This passage will be found on p. 105.

2. See Leslie Hardinge, *The Celtic Church in Britain*, SPCK. London, 1972, pp. 103–5, which sets this out in dialogue, and James Carney. *Medieval Irish Lyrics*, Dolmen Press, Dublin, 1967, pp. 3–7 in poetic form.

144

3. For an interesting discussion of this point see Peter Brown, *The Cult of the Saints*, SCM Press, 1981, pp. 124–5.

4. James Carney ed, *The Poems of Blathmac, son of Cu Brettan*. Irish Texts Society, Dublin, 1966, pp. 65–7.

5. See pp. 122–4.

6. Stokes, *Thesaurus Poleohibernicus* I, 115. I owe this reference to Leslie Hardinge, *The Celtic Church in Britain*, p. 59.

7. E. Hull, *The Poem Book of the Gael*.

8. There are a number of translations of this long poem. The one I have used here is a shortened version taken from Gerard Murphy ed. *Early Irish Lyrics, Eighth to Twelfth Century*, Oxford, 1956, pp. 11–19. The whole is beautifully set out in Ludwig Bieler, *Ireland, Harbinger of the Middle Ages*, London, 1963, pp. 59–61.

9. This is all that remains of a ninth-century lyric by monastic poet. David Green and Frank O'Connor eds *A Golden Treasury of Irish Poetry AD 600–1200*, Macmillan, 1967, p. 101.

10. Robin Flower, "The Two Eyes of Ireland", *Religion and Literature in Ireland AD 432–1932*, Report of the Church of Ireland Conference 1932 ed. William Bell and N. D. Emerson, Dublin, 1932, pp. 66–75.

11. A tenth-century poem attributed to St Manchon, Greene and O'Connor, *A Golden Treasury*. p. 150.

12. Kenneth Jackson, *Studies in Early Celtic Nature Poetry*, Cambridge, 1935. p.3.
For further discussion of this whole subject see Gerard Murphy. "The Origin of Irish Nature Poetry", *Studies, Irish Quarterly Review*, March 1931, xx, No. 77, pp. 87–102.

13. On a visit to his hermitage with Br Patrick Hart a few years ago I was interested to see that amongst the small number of special books kept on a shelf above his desk was a copy of Nora Chadwick's *The Age of the Saints*. He corresponded with her and with Eleanor Duckett, and made Celtic monasticism the subject of his teaching to the novices.

14. John Howard Griffin, *The Hermitage Journals. A Diary kept while working on the Biography of Thomas Merton*, ed. Conger Beasley Jr. Image Books, 1983, pp. 144–5.

15. The most recent study is John J. O'Mearra *Eriguena*, Oxford 1988, which gives a useful summary of his writing.

16. *Carmina Gadelica*. This quotation comes from Catherine Maclennan, the wife of a crofter, III. p. 25.

17. *Carmina Gadelica* III p. 41–7. also *Celtic Vision* pp. 20–22.

18. *Carmina Gadelica* III p. 59, *Celtic Vision* p. 31.

19. *Carmina Gadelica* III p. 43, *Celtic Vision* p. 21.

20. *Carmina Gadelica* I pp. 38–41, *Celtic Vision* p. 29.

21. Ysgubau'r Awen, Llandyseil, 1938, p. 85. I owe this reference to the Rev. Canon A. M. Allchin, and his wide-ranging knowledge of twentieth century Welsh poetry.

22. M. J. Massingham, *The Tree of Life*, London, 1943, p. 40. I owe this reference to Christopher Bamford in his *Heritage of Celtic Christianity*, Lindisfarne Press.

COMMON CREATION

1. Peter O'Dwyer, *Celi De*, p. 140.

2. See Pochin Mould, *Irish Saints*, pp. 110–11.

3. A. W. Wade–Evans, *Vitae Sanctorum*, p.9.

4. See Helen Waddell, trans., *Beasts and Saints*, Constable, 1934, pp. 101–7.

5. *Celtic Christianity, An Anthology*, p. 50.

6. "Life of St Ciaran of Clonmacnois", Stokes, *Book of Lismore*, p. 266.

7. Waddell, *Beasts and Saints*, p. 266.

8. Murphy, *Early Irish Lyrics* p.2. I have used the translation by Robin Flower in *The Irish Tradition*, Oxford, 1947.

9. Wade-Evans, *Vitae Sanctorum*, p.13.

10. *Ibid.*, p. 288.

11. Plummer, *Lives of Irish Saints*, p. 28.

12. See the article by Sr Benedicta Ward already referred to in note 22, on p. 143.

13. I owe this reference to Fr. Martin Smith SSJE.

14. Quoted V. Lossky, *Mystical Theology of the Eastern Church*, London, 1957, p. 111.

HEALING

1. *Carmina Gadelica*, IV, p. 131.

2. *Ibid.*, II p.78.

3. The full text of this has been given already on pp. 78–9.

4. *Ibid.*, II pp. 104–5.

5. *Ibid.*, IV pp. 132–5.

6. James Carney ed. *Blathmac*, pp. 11–15, Shortened.

7. *Ibid.*, II p.95

8. *Ibid.*, II p. 185.

9. *Ibid.*, p. 163

10. Wade-Evans, *Vitae Sanctorum*, p.95.

11. Lady Gregory, *A Book of Saints and Wonders*, Colin Smythe, 1973, p. 12.

SIN AND SORROW

1. Seamus Heaney, *Preoccupations, Selected Prose 1968–1978*, Faber, 1980, p.189.

2. *The Whole Earth Shall Cry Glory, Iona Prayers by the Rev. George F. MacLeod*, Wild Goose Publications, 1985, p.8.

3. Murphy, ed. *Early Irish Lyrics*, pp. 51–3.

4. *Lives of The Irish Saints*, "The Twelve Apostles of Ireland," pp. 96–7.

5. All these references I owe to the article "The Celtic Monk at Prayer" by Diarmuid O'Laoghaire SJ. in *Monastic Studies*, 14 1983, p. 12.

6. Murphy, ed. *Early Irish Lyrics*, p. 63.

7. This although attributed to the sixth century St. Ciaran is clearly a few centuries later. Plummer ed. *Irish Litanies* pp. 2–7. I owe this to Diarmuid O'Laoghaire *op. cit.*, pp. 135–6. The threefold mansion which is mentioned is a reference to heaven, earth and hell.

8. J. McNeill, *History of the Cure of Souls*, Columbia, 1938, p.116.

9. This is probably a ninth-century text, and again something that I owe to Diarmuid O'Laoghaire, p. 137.

10. L. Bieler, *Irish Penitentials*, Dublin Institute of Advanced Studies, 1963, p. 99.

11. The section on martyrdom owes much to two articles, Clare Stancliffe, "Red, white and blue martyrdom", in *Ireland in Early Medieval Europe, Studies in memory of Kathleen Hughes*, ed. D. White-lock, R. McKitterick and D. Dumville, Cambridge 1981, pp. 21–46, and A.M. Allchin, "Martyrdom," *Sobornost*, 1984, Vol. 6 pp. 19–22.

SALVATION

1. Translation by Mrs C. F. Alexander.
2. I owe this phrase to Robin Flower in his article "Irish High Crosses", *Journal of The Warburg and Courtauld Institutes*, vol. XVII, 1954, Nos 1–2, p. 91.
3. Another quotation from Diarmuid O'Laoghaire p.130. W. Stokes and K. Meyer, *Archiv für Celtische Lexicographie*, III, 232.
4. Whitley Stokes, *Felure Oengusso*, Henry Bradshaw Society, XXIX, 1905, Quoted Flower, *op. cit.*, pp. 91–2.
5. M. Maher, ed. *Irish Spirituality*, Veritas, Dublin, 1981, pp. 17–18.

THE CROSS

1. See the pamphlet by Eoin de Bhaldraithe "The High Crosses of Moone and Castledermot", published by Bolton Abbey, Moon.
2. The best studies of the high crosses are to be found in Françoise Henry, *Irish High Crosses*, published for the Cultural Relations Committee of Ireland, Dublin, 1964, and *Irish Art during the Viking Invasions AD 800–1200*, Methuen, London, 1967, Chapter 5.
See also Hilary Richardson "Concept of the High Cross, Irland und Europa, Ireland and Europe". The Early Church, Poirsea Ni Chatha', Michael Ritter, Stuttgart, 1984. There is an interesting discussion by Ciaran O'Sabhaios OCSO "Irish High Crosses and a Hunger cloth from Haiti", in *Monastic Studies*, 14, 1983. pp. 51–63.
3. In an article already referred to in "Salvation" footnote 2.
4. See p. 114.
5. *Blathmac*, pp. 17–21, shortened.
6. Kuno Meyer, *Ancient Irish Poetry*, p. 99.
7. Douglas Hyde, *Religious Songs*, II, pp. 34–5.
8. *Ibid.*, II p.9.
9. *Ibid.*, II p. 359.
10. *Ibid.*, II p. x
11. Hyde II, p. 287.
12. *Carmina Gadelica* III, p. 103, *Celtic Vision* p. 162.
13. *Carmina Gadelica* III, p. 93 *Celtic Vision* p. 167.

14. *Carmina Gadelica* III, 99–101. *Celtic Vision* p. 166.
15. Hyde, II p. 395.
16. Hyde II p. 227.

A WORLD MADE WHOLE

1. Gwenallt, *Eples*, Gomer Press, 1951, pp. 63–4.
2. Part of a poem by Dafydd ap Gwilym c. 1320–80 Gwyn Williams, *Introduction to Welsh Poetry*, Faber, 1953, pp. 49–50.
3. Euros Bowen, *Detholion Yr Academi Cymraeg*, 1984 p. 199. I owe this translation to the Rev. James Coutts.
4. Quoted Roger Corless "Fire on the Seven Storey mountain", *Towards an Integrated Humanity: Thomas Merton's Journey*, Cistercian Publications, Kalamazoo, 1988, p. 209.
5. Adomnan's Life of St Columba p. 219, p. 473.
6. Hughes, *Celtic Monasticism*, p. 4.
7. Plummer, *Lives of The Irish Saints*, I, p. 49.
8. Plummer II p. 288.
9. Hyde, I, p. 319.
10. Cynthia Bourgeault, see article already referred to on p. 145.
11. T. E. Ellis and J. H. Davies, *Gweithiau Morgan Llwyd*, Bangor, University of Wales Press 1899, Vol I p. 188. I owe this reference to the Rev. Saunders Davies.
12. E. Hull, *Poem Book*, .
13. *Agenda*, ed. William Cookson, Vol. 11–12, 1973–4, p.33
14. *The Primal Vision. Christian Presence Amid African Religion*, SCM, 1963, p. 187.
15. See F. Henry, *Irish Art* pp. 68–94. See also Peter Brown *The Book of Kells*, Thames and Hudson 1980.
16. F. Henry, *Early Christian Irish Art*, published for the Cultural Relations Committee of Ireland, Cork, 1979, p.43.